CU00407873

THE SHROPSHIRE WAY
and
Wild Edric's Way

The Feathers, Ludlow

THE SHROPSHIRE WAY
and
Wild Edric's Way

by

TERRY MARSH
and
JULIE MEECH

CICERONE PRESS
MILNTHORPE, CUMBRIA

© Terry Marsh and Julie Meech, 1999
All photographs: © Julie Meech
Maps by Martin Collins
ISBN 1 85284 281 4

First published 1999

A catalogue record for this book is available from the British Library.

ACKNOWLEDGEMENTS

They'll be glad to hear the last of us, but the Rights of Way Officers of Shropshire County Council have been immensely helpful in dealing with the numerous problems we raised at a time when their resources were very limited. We much appreciated their help and co-operation.

Unacknowledged poetry quotations are from *A Shropshire Lad*, with grateful thanks to the Society of Authors, as the Literary Representative of the Estate of A. E. Housman, for permission to use the quotations.

Front cover: On Stiperstones (Julie Meech)

CONTENTS

ADVICE TO READERS

Readers are advised that while every effort has been taken by the authors to ensure the accuracy of this guidebook, changes can occur which may affect the contents. It is advisable to check locally on transport, accommodation, shops, etc., but even rights of way can be altered, or paths affected by erosion, fires or changes of ownership.

The publishers would welcome notes of any such changes.

Warning: There are a number of sections of the Shropshire Way that are frequently overgrown or cropped over, and paths may be obstructed by electric fencing. This is illegal, but it happens, and compels walkers to take evasive action.

If you encounter any such obstruction, please report it to the Rights of Way Officer, Shropshire County Council, Countryside Service, Shire Hall, Abbey Foregate, Shrewsbury, Shropshire SY2 6ND. If you can supply grid references and a photograph, so much the better.

This guidebook has been produced in accordance with the guidelines for writers of path guides produced by the Outdoor Writers' Guild.

THE SHROPSHIRE WAY

INTRODUCTION

The original line of the Shropshire Way was devised by members of various Shropshire rambling groups in 1979/80, and a guide to the route first published in 1981. A revised version appeared in 1991, and even more revision came about in 1995. Quite why so much change was needed may not be immediately apparent, but suffice to say that what exists now, with a few minor modifications that it has been necessary for us to accommodate, should be regarded as the definitive route, unlikely to need further change.

In 1980, the Way began in the north of the county, and linked with the Sandstone Trail near Whitchurch, before taking a circular course south of Shrewsbury. Later, the present circular format appeared, starting and finishing in Shrewsbury, and incorporating what was known as the Clun Extension.

Previously, the section through Bishop's Castle and Clun had not featured in the walk, and a more direct route was taken from Bridges to Hopesay. In this edition, we have omitted the direct route altogether since we no longer see any justification for it.

The Northern Extension, between Wem and Grindley Brook, which connects with the Sandstone Trail, appears as a separate section, and enables walkers to lengthen the route by twenty-four miles (starting and finishing at Grindley Brook) and to include the town of Whitchurch, if they wish.

We have elected, however, to begin the walk in Shrewsbury, the county town. It is well served by public transport and has a wide range of facilities and amenities. We have divided the walk into three sections. This is purely for convenience and has no other significance. Section 1 ends at Ludlow, Section 2 at Ironbridge and Section 3 back in Shrewsbury. In between you travel some of the most inspiring, and least publicised, countryside in England, on footpaths that guide you through pastoral and upland landscapes, wooded dingles and lofty ridges, along river valleys, over wind-swept summits, and through towns and villages of considerable antiquity and interest.

But there is far more to Shropshire than that; as you will see.

For good measure, this guide includes another local walk of some fascination – Wild Edric's Way – much of which coincides with the Shropshire Way, but with sufficient of its own identity to make it a worthwhile, but much shorter, walk. Wild Edric's Way begins in Church Stretton, sweeps over the heights of Long Mynd, much as Wild Edric himself did, and then drops to meet the Shropshire Way at Bridges. Its final destination is Ludlow.

Walkers with limited experience of long-distance walking may find Wild Edric's Way a useful introduction before tackling the Shropshire Way in its entirety.

SHROPSHIRE PROFILE

Once in the wind of morning
I ranged the thymy wold;
The world-wide air was azure
And all the brooks ran gold

It must say something about the scenic, cultural and historical wealth of a county if, in the process of sustaining an outstanding long-distance walk, it can afford to leave out such gems as Bridgnorth, the Stretton Hills, the Long Mynd and a host of sequestered villages set among emerald green hills. These places alone are justification for any walker coming to Shropshire; the Shropshire Way is very much the icing on the perambulatory cake.

Shropshire, a county almost divided in two by Britain's longest river, the Severn, is a place of endless fascination. Its landscape is varied and beautiful, and it has played a part in English history since Roman times. And yet among the walking fraternity it is sadly neglected and under-rated, an oversight that needs to be redressed. Both of us have walked extensively throughout the British Isles, in France and Spain, and much further afield – Africa, Australia and New Zealand. But the buxom, bosomy hills of Shropshire remain no less exciting and welcoming, and it is always a pleasure to sink into the flowing folds of this exquisite landscape.

What makes Shropshire so special is, of course, its underlying geology, which is both unique and complex. Geologists venture that there is no other comparable area of England where the rock formations are so varied. They range from the pre-Cambrian rocks of the Wrekin to the limestone outcrops of Wenlock Edge, from the sandstone of northern Shropshire to the coalfields of the east.

North of the River Severn the land is an undulating plain, ideal for arable and dairy farming. To the south it is just as green and luxurious, dotted with scattered villages and small farming communities that flourish in the fertile valleys, but it's wonderfully hilly too, with some rugged and very distinctive uplands, where sheep outnumber people and the walking opportunities are first class. A large part of this area is designated the Shropshire Hills Area of Outstanding Natural Beauty.

Much of the development of the county has been influenced to varying degrees by the Severn. It is unquestionably one of the principal characters of Shropshire, though the Shropshire Way spends but little time in its company. The river was (and is) known as Hafren to the Celts, but called 'Sabrina' by the Romans, after the daughter of Locrine, a king of Loegria, and Estrildis, his mistress. Legend tells how Locrine's wife, Queen Gwendolen, angered by her husband's deceit, drowned both Sabrina and her mother in the river.

As elsewhere in Britain, the first hunter-gatherers to venture into the region would have found it densely wooded and inhospitable, and the evidence of the earliest prehistoric remains suggests no more than trade routes through the county. A good number of Bronze Age sites have been identified, but it was not until the Iron Age that the region became inhabited to any substantial extent. About twenty-five hill-forts survive from this period, and the Shropshire Way passes through several, two of the most notable being Bury Ditches on Sunnyhill and another on the Wrekin that is believed to have been the regional 'capital' of the Cornovii, a Celtic people who came to control much of what is now Shropshire.

The hill-forts were sacked by the Romans, who established a camp, Viroconium, by the Severn, at what is now Wroxeter. It served as a military base for thirty years, until superseded by Chester, when it developed into a substantial town. Further north, another Roman military camp developed into Mediolanum, a thriving regional centre that was later to become known as Whitchurch. The Romans knew the importance of communications and the roads they built through Shropshire are mostly still in use, though in a modern guise.

Following the departure of the Romans, the Dark Ages that followed were especially dark in Shropshire, with tribal strife the overwhelming theme. The remoteness of the region was a significant feature in delaying the advance of the invading Anglo-Saxon forces but as they did push slowly westwards they met with fierce resistance from the retreating Celts and it was not until the seventh century that they established anything approaching control. The most outstanding legacy of these times, apart from some fine examples of Saxon church architecture, is that massive rampart, Offa's Dyke, the construction of which was ordered in AD779 by Offa, King of Mercia from AD757 to 796. Today, the dyke represents something of an enigma. Nobody really knows why Offa should have wanted it; some see it as the first serious attempt to establish a permanent fortified boundary with Wales, but most experts consider that it was intended merely to define the boundary, and may also have served as a sort of customs barrier where tolls were imposed on cross-border trade. Whatever its purpose, it was a magnificent achievement and the Shropshire Way makes a brief visit to it near Bishop's Castle.

The Norman name for the county was 'Salopescire', which gave rise to the name 'Salop', a synonym adopted at the time of local government reform in 1974 but cast aside by the county council in 1980 when it decided to use the traditional form. At the time of the Domesday survey, however, the shape of Shropshire was considerably different from its present form. Parts belonged to what are now Herefordshire, Staffordshire and Worcestershire, and the border with Wales was not clearly defined.

Following the Norman Conquest the three principal English border counties were governed by some of William I's most trusted lieutenants and formed a buffer between England and Wales known as the Marches. William needed a strong military presence along the border and in return for providing this the Marcher lords were granted an unusual degree of autonomy. Most of Shropshire was ruled by Roger de Montgomery and his descendants from their base at Shrewsbury, while Roger de Lacy and his family held sway at Ludlow before it passed into the hands of the powerful Mortimers. Numerous other lords ruled their own lesser territories from strategically sited castles. For nearly 400 years these Marcher lords dominated the borders. They ruled as they pleased, building numerous castles to overawe the local population, to defend against the Welsh and to provide places of refuge when their own internecine squabbling broke out into more serious fighting. The castles began life as simple motte and bailey fortifications, about 150 being built altogether, and traces are still to be found in a number of villages. More important castles were later rebuilt in stone (Ludlow is rare in having been built in stone from the first) and some substantial ruins survive.

But castles aren't the only legacy from these times – Shropshire also delights in an unusually high number of Norman churches, a constant source of interest to modern-day visitors. Some of them have square, sturdy towers clearly demonstrating that they, too, were at times used defensively, as places of refuge for villagers threatened by raiding parties. Many of them occupy circular churchyards, usually considered a sign that the site had some pre-Christian religious significance.

Later, when the medieval open fields were being enclosed, it was largely done by the traditional method of using trees and hedges, with very few drystone walls. In places today, where these ancient hedgerows have been grubbed out, it is often only the few trees that remain that survive to indicate where the boundaries once lay. But while many old hedgerows have disappeared from the north of the county, in the south, where the need for large open pastures is much less, there are still some magnificent hedgerows to be found. Large areas of common land, too, are a notable feature of Shropshire, though, in spite of its numerous villages, there are surprisingly few with greens.

Shropshire is perhaps the most deeply rural of all English counties, yet it was here that the first stirrings of the Industrial Revolution were felt and, for a time, the Ironbridge Gorge was the foremost industrial area in the world. The gorge is green and wooded again but the legacy of that time is an endlessly fascinating collection of early industrial remains, most of which lie close to the Shropshire Way as it travels between Benthall Edge and Little Wenlock.

Yet the present landscape is quite simply enchanting, and the contrasts experienced as you walk along the Way do much to maintain a fascination with the county that begins the moment you arrive. There is constant change; each mile upon mile has something different from those before; each hour that passes brings new sights and new delights.

And above all else is the invigorating air, the home of the buzzard that has become the symbol of the Shropshire Way. It is unlikely that you will spend a day on the walk without sight of a buzzard, and if you do, then you'll certainly make up for it later. For the buzzards are everywhere, and everywhere a pleasure to see, and a joy to hear. Their call is one of freedom, an appropriate call for those about to venture into their country.

EXPLANATORY NOTES
Direction and route description

Being a circular walk it is, of course, possible to walk the Shropshire Way in either a clockwise or an anticlockwise direction. There is really nothing to choose between them: clockwise begins with the pastoral landscapes of north Shropshire and concludes with a splendid romp from Ludlow to Clun, Bishop's Castle and back to Shrewsbury. The anticlockwise direction does the opposite.

Because the route involves much linking of farms and pastures, to-ing and fro-ing around the fascinating hills, and diving into and climbing out of valleys, we have chosen to provide what in effect are two standards of description. The anticlockwise direction contains full background information and notes, and here the route description is given in full detail. The clockwise direction, however, does not contain the background information, etc. (though it is cross-referenced), and its route description is less detailed. Walkers wanting clear guidance, therefore, should opt for the anticlockwise direction; those wanting something a little more adventurous should go clockwise.

While the Shropshire Way is unquestionably a walk to rank alongside the finest in Britain, it is, for the time being, less well known and much less travelled than others. As a result, the basic infrastructure, especially in terms of accommodation and camping sites, is not directly linked to the Way, but rather it is geared to accommodating visitors on holiday in Shropshire. Likewise, a number of the paths are less well trodden, have rickety stiles, and in some cases are poorly waymarked. Nor is it unusual to find field paths cropped over, facing you with the dilemma of either trampling through crops, or trying to find a way around the headland – which itself can be difficult.

[NOTE: Trying to deal with cropped-over rights of way has a number of legal implications. If the obstruction (i.e. the cropping) is by the holder of the land, there is undoubtedly a right to deviate onto other land belonging to the same landholder in order to get round the obstruction. It is therefore acceptable in law that if a cross-field path has been ploughed or disturbed, and a walker goes round the edge to avoid the difficulties this presents, no trespass is committed.

Similarly, if crops are of a kind, or of a height, that makes it difficult to follow the correct line of the right of way, they constitute an obstacle that entitles the walker to deviate around the edge of the field. The Ramblers' Association and the Open Spaces Society, however, take the view that unless crops present a severe obstacle, the legal line of the right of way across a field should be followed.]

From another point of view this is one of the attractions of the Way, since it imposes on the walker a keener sense of self-dependence and self-reliance, and that is no bad thing. It is conceivable, but unlikely, that you could walk the whole of the Way, and not meet another soul.

Distances

To ensure accuracy when giving distances, detailed measurements have been made using OS Pathfinder Maps, at a scale of 1:25000, where necessary, measuring distances at 100-metre intervals. There is inevitably a lack of precision in this, and our measurement of distances may differ slightly from the official distances; any such discrepancy, however, is unlikely to be significant.

Using the guide

Following this brief section of explanatory notes the guide is divided into a number of sections. The first is advice on how to go about planning the walk and about walking it. The second section is the route description given in an anticlockwise direction, the third the route description given in a clockwise direction, and the fourth a list of what we regard as essential and supplementary reading, some or all of which will enhance your experience of the walk.

Finally, there is an accommodation listing. This can never be complete since the Shropshire Way is a developing tourist industry of its own, and changes occur each year. If you find somewhere that is good, and not listed, please drop us a line via the publishers so that we can include the address in any revision of the guide.

In the text the main route description and authors' comments are given in normal type, while observations and general background information are given in italics. These occur in the main text in the order in which they are encountered along the walk. Observations and background information in the clockwise direction is absent, but there is a page number cross-reference (e.g. Haughmond Abbey (123)) so that you can find the appropriate reference in the main text.

Although the route description is written in three sections, no attempt has been made to construct 'day length' sections – that is for you to do, but please be sure not to overstretch yourself. The Shropshire Way is immensely pleasurable, but not when you are weary.

Keep it simple; keep it within your capability.

PLANNING THE WALK
Preparation and fitness

Fit, healthy and experienced visitors accustomed to long days of walking will encounter no difficulty in tackling the Shropshire Way, but it would be foolish even to think about setting off if you have not previously done any rough walking or had to carry heavy packs. Getting yourself into condition is neither an arduous nor an unpleasant process, and every walk you do in preparation will make your experience and enjoyment of the Way all the better.

Nor does conditioning extend only to you. It is vitally important, for example, that you avoid wearing new boots that are not broken in or clothing that has not had the chance to lose its newness. Comfort on a long walk can be critically important; discomfort can be painful if allowed to go on too long. If you do feel blisters coming on, or your boots start rubbing, do attend to the problem sooner rather than later.

When to do it

Many people, perhaps because of family or work commitments and obligations, may have little freedom over when they choose to tackle a long walk. But, if possible, there are certain times to be avoided, sometimes for less obvious reasons than the congestion you can expect during the main tourist months of July and August. Certainly, if you can avoid these months, you are less likely to find accommodation fully booked. This is especially important on the Shropshire Way, where accommodation in places is sparse. In any event, it is always wise to plan your route carefully and to book accommodation well ahead.

Maps

Until the Ordnance Survey completes development of its Explorer Series of maps (during 1999 for Shropshire), walkers on the Shropshire Way will find they need quite a bagful of OS Pathfinder Maps. These are (with the new Explorer numbers):

807 (257)*:	Whitchurch (Shropshire) and Malpas (Cheshire)
828 (241)*:	Ellesmere (East) and Prees
848 (241):	Wem and Myddle
869 (241):	Shrewsbury
870 (242):	Telford (North)
889 (241):	Dorrington and Cressage
890 (242):	Ironbridge and Telford (South)
909 (216):	Montgomery
910 (217):	Church Stretton
911 (217):	Bridgnorth and Much Wenlock
930 (216/201):	Bishop's Castle and Clun
931 (217):	Craven Arms
932 (217):	Highley
951 (203):	Ludlow

* Needed only by walkers including the northern link to the Sandstone Trail

Daily itineraries

These are really a bit of a nonsense, because you must plan your daily walk according to your own strengths and abilities, and not according to some vague plan we might suggest. The basic circuit is 217.5km (136 miles) in length, which ideally gives ten days of about 22km (13¾ miles). Most people would find this comfortable, but that makes no allowance for rest (or easy) days, or exploring off-route. Nor does the Shropshire Way conform to such mathematical precision. The section from Ludlow to Wilderhope Manor is rather longer (31.5km / 19½ miles) than others; there used to be a youth hostel at Wheathill, but this closed in 1998.

Start	8 days	10 days	12 days
Shrewsbury	Bridges	Bridges	Bridges
Bridges	Clun	Bishop's Castle	Bishop's Castle
Bishop's Castle		Clun	Clun
Clun	Ludlow	Craven Arms	Craven Arms
Craven Arms		Ludlow	Ludlow
Ludlow	Wilderhope	Wilderhope	Wilderhope
Wilderhope	Ironbridge	Ironbridge	Much Wenlock
Much Wenlock			Ironbridge
Ironbridge	High Ercall	High Ercall	High Ercall
High Ercall	Grinshill	Wem	Wem
Wem		Shrewsbury	Grinshill
Grinshill	Shrewsbury		Shrewsbury

The Shropshire Way, however, is not a forced march, something you have to do in so many days (unless, of course, commitments mean that you do). The Way is a walk to be enjoyed leisurely; something to take your time over and to use as a gateway to exploration of the countryside that lies to either side of it.

Accommodation

The walk is never far from civilisation, but it is not well supported by accommodation throughout its entire length. So don't take accommodation for granted; book ahead, a day at a time may suffice at quiet times of the year. In the main tourist season, however, there is pressure on all the accommodation along the Way, while in the quieter months some closes down altogether.

The range of accommodation is much the same as elsewhere. In addition to the B&Bs, guest houses, hotels and campsites that you would expect, the Way also boasts seven good youth hostels ideally placed for Wayfarers.

Public Transport

The Shropshire Way is easily reached by public transport, whether you choose to travel by train, coach or bus. Shrewsbury has the best connections, with frequent train services from Birmingham, operated by Central Trains, and on the Manchester-Cardiff line, operated by Wales and West. Virgin Trains operates a direct Intercity service from London, and Central provides regular services from Chester. Visitors from Wales are not restricted to services from Cardiff; they also have the option of the highly scenic Heart of Wales line (Wales and West) from Swansea, and the Cambrian Coaster (Central Trains) from Pwllheli, Aberystwyth and Machynlleth.

Shrewsbury is also easily, cheaply and reliably accessible by National Express coach services, which operate daily along three routes: London to Shrewsbury (520), London to Wrexham via Shrewsbury (521) and London to Aberystwyth via Shrewsbury (522).

Shrewsbury is the county's main hub for local bus services, which operate from all over Shropshire and also from neighbouring counties; for instance, there are regular services from towns and cities such as Llanidloes, Newtown, Welshpool, Hanley, Stoke-on-Trent and Birmingham. It's worth noting, however, that Sunday services are very sparse.

Walkers starting at Grindley Brook can reach it by using buses on the Chester-Malpas-Whitchurch route, currently operated by Chester City Transport and Huxleys Coaches on Mondays to Saturdays. However, nearby Whitchurch is served by daily trains on the Manchester-Cardiff line and many walkers will find it a more convenient starting point than Grindley Brook. Whitchurch is also served by local buses, with services from many places. The most frequent are those from Shrewsbury, Nantwich and Market Drayton, and there are also buses from Hanley, Oswestry, Wrexham and Telford.

If you do arrive at Whitchurch you can take a bus to Grindley Brook, or you can walk there along the towpath of the Llangollen

Canal. From the station the best route is as follows: Station Road, Green End, Mill Street then Wharf Park Avenue into Jubilee Park. Cross the park to Sherrymill Hill, turn left and keep straight on to the curiously named Chemistry, where access to the Whitchurch Arm of the canal will soon be found on the right. When the arm joins the main canal a right turn should be made to reach Grindley Brook. However, for those with no particular desire to visit Grindley Brook, a left turn will enable you to join the Shropshire Way near Blackoe Cottages.

Those of you preferring to walk the Shropshire Way in short stages, or who intend only to sample parts of it on day walks, will find no difficulty in accessing the greater part of the route by public transport. Shrewsbury and Whitchurch are not the only train stations in the county – stations at Ludlow, Craven Arms, Church Stretton, Prees, Wem, Yorton, and Wellington are all on, or very close to, the Shropshire Way.

National Express coaches stop at Telford, which is handy for connections to Ironbridge (trains call at Telford too, but Wellington Station is closer to the Way).

Local buses reach many of the areas that trains and coaches don't penetrate, and offer greater flexibility. Ludlow is the main hub for South Shropshire, with many useful services. One that deserves special mention is the 192/292 from Hereford to Birmingham via Ludlow and Cleehill. It's enormously useful and operates daily, though with only a sparse service on Sundays. Wellington and Telford enjoy a good range of services too, many operating from such centres of population as Wolverhampton and Stafford, and connecting with buses for Ironbridge.

Information about public transport is easy to find. Shropshire County Council has a telephone enquiry line and publishes free timetable books that cover the county area by area. You can pick these up at tourist information centres, council offices, libraries and bus station travel centres (at Shrewsbury, Telford and Oswestry). Copies may also be obtained direct from the county council and the address is given below. The aim is to revise the booklets at least once a year, but monthly updates detailing any changes are also published. Changes are announced on local radio too. Individual travel operators also have enquiry lines and publish their own timetable leaflets. In addition, many libraries, tourist information centres, travel centres and rail stations have copies of the National Express Timetable and the very useful Great Britain Bus Timetable, also available on subscription from the publishers, Southern Vectis Bus Company (which operates the TBC Hotline).

Because there are so many different travel operators serving Shropshire it would be impractical to list them all here. However, any information you need may be obtained from ringing one of the telephone numbers listed below. Timetables and other information are also available on the Internet.

Useful telephone numbers
Shropshire Traveline 0345 056785 (0800-1800 Mon-Sat)
Cheshire Busline 01244 602666 (0800-1800 Mon-Fri; 0900-1300 Sat)
National Express 0990 808080 (0800-2000 daily)
National Rail Enquiries 0345 484950 (24 hours daily)
TBC (Train, Bus and Coach) Hotline 0891 910910 (0600-2100 daily)

Useful addresses
Public Transport Unit
Shropshire County Council
The Shirehall
Abbey Foregate
Shrewsbury SY2 6ND

Southern Vectis Bus Company
Nelson Road
Newport
Isle of Wight PO30 1RD

Equipment
All walkers have their own preferences in the matter of equipment and clothing. When extending day walking into multiple day walking much the same general items are needed, with the emphasis on being able to stay warm and dry (as much as possible), and comfortable in all weather conditions.

The following list may be found a useful reminder – rucksack (comfortable, well padded, appropriate to backpacking rather than day walking, and preferably already used by you, if only on trial walks), boots, socks (and spare socks), trousers (or shorts, etc., but not shorts alone – at certain times of the year there are a lot of nettles), underclothes, shirt, midwear (e.g. pullover) and spare, wind- or waterproof jacket and overtrousers, hat, gloves, maps, compass, torch (with spare battery and bulbs), whistle, first aid kit, survival bag or space blanket, food and drink, insect repellent, ablution tackle, including half a roll of toilet tissue (for emergencies), small hand towel.

Campers will also need such additional weighty items as tent, sleeping bag, Karrimat, cooking equipment and utensils.

Pedal bin liners will be found to have a number of useful purposes: keeping wet clothes separate from dry in the sack, containing burst packets of food, etc., and rubbish, until a suitable disposal point can be reached, and for insulating dry socks from wet boots when walking.

With few opportunities along the Way to obtain cash, it becomes vitally important that you estimate your money requirements in advance. There are banks in Shrewsbury, Bishop's Castle, Clun, Craven Arms and Ludlow, but after that nothing until Much Wenlock, Ironbridge and Wem. A cheque book and banker's card can often be used to obtain cash from post offices that are scattered about the various villages. But the best advice is that if you need cash be sure to get it in the main towns.

Useful addresses

Tourist Information Centres on, or close to, the Shropshire Way:
CHURCH STRETTON
The Library, Church Street, Church Stretton SY6 6DQ.
Tel: 01694 723133
IRONBRIDGE
The Wharfage, Ironbridge TF8 7AW.
Tel: 01952 432166
LUDLOW
Castle Street, Ludlow SY8 1AS.
Tel: 01584 875053
MUCH WENLOCK
The Museum, High Street, Much Wenlock TF13 6HR.
Tel: 01952 727679

SHREWSBURY
The Music Hall, The Square, Shrewsbury SY1 1LH.
Tel: 01743 350761
WHITCHURCH
Heritage Centre, 12 St Mary's Street, Whitchurch SY13 1QY.
Tel: 01948 664577

In addition to Tourist Information Centres, Shropshire has a network of Tourist Information Points (TIPs), all located in small, privately owned businesses. They provide local information and a list of serviced accommodation, but are not authorised to make bed bookings, and only the one at Bishop's Castle can deal with telephone enquiries.

BISHOP'S CASTLE
Old Time, 29 High Street, Bishop's Castle.
Tel: 01588 638467
BROMFIELD
The Cook House, The Clive Arms, Bromfield.
CLEEHILL
Post Office Stores, Cleehill.
CLUN
The Clun Garage, Clun.
CRAVEN ARMS
The Paper Shop, Corvedale Road, Craven Arms.
HADNALL
Post Office Stores, Hadnall
LYDHAM
Harvest Wholefoods, Lydham.
MUCH WENLOCK
Wenlock Books, Much Wenlock.
ONIBURY
Post Office Stores, Onibury.
WEM
Martins the Newsagents, Wem.

SHROPSHIRE WAY (Anticlockwise)

SECTION 1: SHREWSBURY TO LUDLOW

Once beyond the suburbs of Shrewsbury the Way suddenly plunges you into the most delightful countryside, climbing steadily to the top of Lyth Hill, a fine vantage point, before threading a way through farmland. Beyond Wilderley Hall Farm the landscape changes slightly as you descend from the Portway, a prehistoric trackway, into the Golden Valley, aptly named when the gorse is in bloom, and on towards Ratlinghope and Bridges.

The ridge of Stiperstones – an outstanding upland divide, crested by crazily pinnacled rocky tors – introduces you to the characteristic undulating nature of the southern part of the Way, where new and alluring vistas open up at every rise and round each turn in the trail.

Gradually you descend to the lovely market town of Bishop's Castle, well able to look after visiting walkers, and continue to yet another delight, the small town of Clun, where each May Day sees the re-enactment of an ancient tradition (and a few newer traditions) on Green Man Day. The castle, too, is well worth a visit.

Beyond Clun, the Way heads initially northwards to visit the magnificent Bury Ditches hill-fort on Sunnyhill, before striking east and south-east for the splendour of Stokesay Castle, and the amenities of Craven Arms. Beyond that it isn't long before the tower of St Laurence's Church in Ludlow appears on the distant skyline, and proves a torment that never seems to come nearer. But, of course, it does, as the Way visits first Onibury and then Stanton Lacy, before the final fling across farmland into Ludlow itself.

SHREWSBURY TO BRIDGES
Distance: 25.75km (16 miles)

High the vanes of Shrewsbury gleam
Islanded in Severn stream;
The bridges from the steepled crest
Cross the water east and west.

Shrewsbury

It was the River Severn which determined Shrewsbury's siting, its development and, to a large extent, its present character. The site of the present town is believed to have been originally the Celtic Pengwern but by 901 we have the first written reference to Scrobbesbyrig – meaning 'the fortified place of Scrob'. Historians are unsure whether 'Scrob' was a personal name or a reference to a scrub-covered hill. Whatever its name meant, Saxon Scrobbesbyrig was built in a tight loop of the Severn, completely encircled except for a 300m/yds gap, making a perfect defensive site. Even the gap was guarded by a ridge, on which a castle was later built.

Soon after the Conquest King William gave much of Shropshire to Roger de Montgomery, the recently created Earl of Shrewsbury, who didn't endear himself to the townsfolk when he had fifty houses demolished to make room for the above-mentioned castle. For years the town was a base for Norman operations against the Welsh, but at the same time it was building on its riverside location to become a busy inland port. By the early fourteenth century it was one of the wealthiest towns in England, largely through its success in the wool trade. It was the wool merchants who built many of the timber-framed mansions which still grace its streets today.

With the decline of the wool trade Shrewsbury reinvented itself as a fashionable centre for leisure and shopping. This role expanded in the great coaching era, thanks to the town's position on the main London-Holyhead route. The coming of the railways killed both road and river traffic but opened up new opportunities. With the subsequent decline of the railways Shrewsbury has become as horribly congested as anywhere else, but remains an important regional centre. For today's visitor, much of its charm derives from the survival of its medieval street pattern, particularly the abundance of narrow passages known locally as shuts and gullets. There's a great deal to see, with a total of 660 Listed Buildings in the town centre alone. Few towns have such an astonishing wealth of period buildings, and the impact is all the greater because most are crowded together in the centre, 'islanded in Severn stream'.

Don't miss the railway station, built of Grinshill stone – with its battlements, pinnacled clock tower and oriel windows this is Victorian 'Tudor' at its most enjoyable. Just a few paces away is the castle – not Roger de Montgomery's original but a later one in red sandstone. Its greatest importance was in the days of cross-border warfare but it was refortified during the Civil War when Charles I established it as a regional headquarters, only to lose it to the Roundheads in 1645. In later years the castle played a variety of roles but is now a regimental museum. The grounds are open daily (except winter Sundays) and you can climb up to Laura's Tower, built by Thomas Telford, and enjoy fine views of the Wrekin. Just across the road is the library, housed in a genuine Tudor building of Grinshill stone, which was the original Shrewsbury School, founded by Edward VI in 1552, before the School moved across the river to Kingsland in 1882. Notable past pupils include Charles Darwin and the Elizabethan soldier-poet Sir Philip Sidney.

Shrewsbury is renowned for its medieval churches. St Mary's, a mixture of many periods, but originally a Saxon foundation, is the largest and best preserved of them. Its fifteenth-century spire, one of the three highest in England, partially collapsed in 1894 but was carefully rebuilt. The vicar was convinced that its collapse was divine retribution, as the townsfolk were at that time organising the erection of a statue of arch-heretic Charles Darwin, which stands outside the library. In 1739 a man called Cadman had attempted to fly from the top of the spire, with predictable results. An entertaining plaque on the tower tells his story.

A quiet corner of Shrewsbury: Old St Chad's churchyard, Belmont

The ancient centre of Shrewsbury is St Alkmund's Square, where there are two more churches of Saxon origin, both rebuilt in the eighteenth century: St Julian's, which now houses a craft market and a restaurant, and St Alkmund's itself. Nearby is a range of timber-framed buildings known as Bear Steps, parts of which date back to the fourteenth century. Neighbouring Butcher Row is worth a look, especially the magnificent Abbot's House of 1450, and so are Fish Street, Dogpole, Wyle Cop, High Street and Milk Street. Wyle Cop, in particular, is lined with marvellous buildings, such as Henry Tudor House, where the future Henry VII stayed one night on his way to victory at Bosworth, and the Lion Hotel, one of many former coaching inns. When the coaching era was at its height, the town provided stabling for over 100 horses a night – many people travelled regularly to London, seemingly undeterred by a journey time approaching thirty hours in 1800. Improved roads had reduced this to sixteen hours by 1831, but in 1849, with the arrival of the railway, London was suddenly a mere five hours away.

Other notable buildings include the ruined church in lovely Belmont, Old St Chad's, and its replacement, New St Chad's, which caused a certain amount of consternation when it was built in 1790-92. Its round nave had some observers tut-tutting that it was more suitable for use as a ballroom. Ireland's Mansion, Owen's Mansion and Rowley's House are all worth seeing – Rowley's is a spectacular timber-framed building in which one William Rowley established himself as a draper and brewer; an odd combination but obviously a successful one, because by 1618 he was prosperous enough to build the attached mansion, the first brick house in Shrewsbury. Today it's open to the public in its new capacity as a museum. Less beautiful, but visible for miles around, is Lord Hill's Column, at the end of Abbey Foregate, completed in 1816 to commemorate the military achievements of Viscount Hill and said to be the tallest Doric column in the world (40m/133ft).

The best place to find out more about Shrewsbury's highlights (and perhaps purchase a town trail booklet) is the Tourist Information Centre in The Square, which itself occupies a fine building, the Music Hall, opposite a delightful Elizabethan Market House.

In the order of things it is probably immaterial exactly where in Shrewsbury you begin the Shropshire Way, but the assumption has been made that the railway station is as good a place as any.

From the station walk up past the castle entrance, and, opposite

Woolworths, turn left into Windsor Place (signposted to the river), and then take the next left, descending St Mary's Water Lane. At the bottom of the lane you reach the River Severn, and turn right on a riverside path. Keep on to pass under English Bridge.

This is just one of several bridges spanning the Severn as it embraces Shrewsbury, but it's probably the most famous as it features in one of the much-photographed classic views of the town. Though the river was bridged at this point by the twelfth century, or even earlier, the present bridge was first completed in 1774, though it was subsequently dismantled in the 1920s and completely reconstructed with a reduced gradient and wider carriageway. Its counterpart on the west side of town is, of course, Welsh Bridge.

At the other side of the bridge is the Wakeman Grammar School, which was built just before the Second World War on the site of the demolished Carlines House. It was originally a technical college, and was attended by Wilfred Owen, the renowned war poet. To its right is the tower of the United Reformed Church, which was built in 1863. Further still to the right is the abbey, the tower of which can be seen above riverside willows.

The abbey, dedicated to St Peter and St Paul, was founded in 1083 by Roger de Montgomery on the site of an earlier Saxon church, just outside the town walls. The abbey church, which survives today, was once part of a much larger complex with a full range of monastic buildings.

Following the Dissolution of the Monasteries, the abbey church survived because it was in use as a parish church, and many of the other buildings survived until 1834 when Thomas Telford drove his Holyhead road through the site, proving that the insensitive vandalism of road-builders is not a new phenomenon. The fourteenth-century refectory pulpit was spared, and now sits incongruously in the middle of a car park across the road. The abbey church contains work from several periods but still retains its massive Norman columns and simple arches. The great west tower was built in the reign of Edward III and is the dominant part of the present building, with the west window considered the finest Perpendicular window in Shropshire. Inside the church is a font made from the base of a Roman pillar from the city of Viroconium.

Keep on beneath a footbridge and continue in company with the river, walking down an avenue of lime trees. The next bridge is Kingsland Bridge, and just as you reach it, turn right on a walled alleyway. At the top of this passage, turn left and double back to cross the bridge.

Opened in 1882 by the Kingsland Bridge Company, the bridge facilitated the move of Shrewsbury School to Kingsland in the same year and helped to establish the area as a wealthy suburb. The iron bridge rests on stone piers and is known locally as Penny Bridge, this being the amount still charged as a pedestrian toll; there's a coin box at the side of the road.

Follow the road beyond to a T-junction, and here cross slightly left into Beehive Lane, a stony track. The lane soon degenerates into a hedged path at the rear of properties, and descends to cross high above a brook, Rad Brook. It then continues as a surfaced path to meet a road.

At the road turn right, cross it and go just past the entrance to a cemetery.

Turn left on an enclosed pathway. This, too, runs on to meet a road. Turn left, and cross the road with great care.

After about 130m/yds leave the road, and descend right, on a signposted path into the edge of a large playing field. Turn left and follow the field boundary, a well-established hawthorn hedgerow, round two sides, as far as a gate giving access to a railway crossing.

Having crossed the railway turn right on a narrow path at the rear of houses. The path brings you out to a road, where you turn left. At a T-junction, 40m/yds later, turn right into Vicarage Road, and when it bends right into Station Road, turn left into Church Road.

This is Meole Brace, which was once part of a vast Royal Forest, but is just another suburb of Shrewsbury now, though the area near the church retains some charm. In the twelfth century the village acquired a castle, erected by the eponymous Norman lord of the manor, de Bracey, but the castle was burnt down in 1669. Holy Trinity Church, built 1867-8, has some superb stained glass designed by Burne-Jones and made by William Morris, and it was in this church that the novelist Mary Webb was married in 1912.

Follow the road round to the edge of a school playing field, and follow a surfaced field-edge path to the far side, turning right near the entrance to Holy Trinity Church. Go past the Meole Brace Infant School, and when the road bends to the right leave it, on the left, going down a surfaced footpath.

Go forward and cross a bridge, and keep on in the same direction beside an iron railing fence to cross Rea Brook, ascending right on the other side.

The Rea Brook Valley has been officially designated a Local Nature Reserve with freely available public access on rights of way and concessionary paths. Managed by Shrewsbury and Atcham Borough Council, it comprises an area of pastures, flood meadows and scrublands along the valley of the Rea Brook from Meole Brace to Abbey Foregate. This delightful green space would probably have fallen prey to the developers had not a survey by Shropshire Wildlife Trust highlighted its great value as a wildlife reservoir and corridor. Some of the valley is farmed but it's done in such a way as to maintain its wildlife value, and much environmental improvement has also been carried out, including the relaying of neglected hedges, the planting of new ones, the reinstatement of traditional tree-management techniques such as pollarding and coppicing and the creation of new wetlands by clearing out silted-up mill leats.

Historically, this land was farmed until the sixteenth century by the monks of Shrewsbury Abbey and it was they who first harnessed the power of the Rea Brook to drive a number of mills. At one time there was a total of six mills between Shrewsbury Abbey and Meole Brace.

When the rising path forks, branch right and soon, at a stile, reach a path around the edge of an arable field. Turn left along this and walk out to a road. Turn right along the road, and, about 40m/yds after crossing the A5, leave the road, on the left, over a stile beside a gate, and go forward along the right-hand field edge. On the far side of the field another stile gives onto a lane at Pulley. Turn right and walk along the lane for 100m/yds, and then leave it, on the left, over a stile. Walk along the left-hand field edge. From the next gate turn right and go to another gate, beyond which you walk up a narrow enclosure, and then keep on in the same direction up the edge of an arable field, following the field edge path round the rear of properties until you can leave the path at a waymarked stile on the right.

Go down between a fence and a hedgerow onto Castle Lane. At the end of the lane, turn right.

Here the Way is travelling through the suburb of Bayston Hill, and the shops offer the last opportunity to buy supplies for some distance.

Bayston Hill was once farmland carved from the forest and for a time coal was dug here from shallow mines. Over the last forty years, however, it has developed into a suburb of Shrewsbury. Few buildings of any interest survive. Even Lythwood Hall, which was designed in the 1780s by George Steuart, also responsible for Attingham Hall (now a National Trust property) near Atcham, has suffered badly from modernisation.

Walk up the road until the main road bends right, and then go forward into the continuation of Lythwood Road.

There are two possibilities now. The apparent line of the Shropshire Way continues up Lythwood Road, but soon leaves it, on the left, at a signposted footpath to find a way past garages and allotments, before closing down into a narrow enclosed pathway. When you are confronted by a stile, go left just before it, over a stile and through a hedgerow, and onto a farm access track. Turn right.

The second, and simpler, possibility takes to the farm access immediately after the main road bend. The two routes combine just before Lythwood Farm.

Go through the farmyard and on the other side forward along a broad track. When the track forks, branch left through a gate and then walk beside a post and wire fence. When the fence meets a hedgerow, stay with the fence, going left, and when this comes to an end, at a fence junction, keep forward across an arable field.

The path eventually brings you out to meet a lane close by a reservoir compound. Turn right along a broad, stony track open to traffic that leads on to Lyth Hill car park and the hill's fine viewpoint just beyond. Parallel with this a path runs through a fenced hill pasture, which is a popular spot for people exercising their dogs. When the track forks, near a radio mast, branch left to reach a toposcope.

Lyth Hill is the first high ground of the Shropshire Way. The view from the top of this modest hill (169m/557ft) is superb, a surprise panorama of what Shropshire novelist Mary Webb described as the 'blue ring of hills' and the 'multiple-tinted, magical' plain. Behind you, to the left, is the Wrekin; when you ultimately reach it you will be more than two-thirds of the distance around the Way. Further right are the Severn Gorge, the low, wooded scarp of Wenlock Edge, Brown Clee, the Stretton Hills, the Long Mynd and Stiperstones.

Mary Webb was born Mary Gladys Meredith at Leighton in 1881. She had a nomadic childhood, her family moving several times. In 1902 they went to live at Meole Brace, where she remained until her marriage to schoolmaster Henry Webb in 1912. Mary was a great walker and during those years at Meole Brace her favourite walk was along the Rea Brook then across the fields and through Pulley to Lyth Hill, where she was enchanted not only by the view but also by Spring Coppice, which she called Little Wood. Later, in 1917, after her first novel had been published, she and Henry bought a plot of land on the hill and Spring Cottage was built for them. This was Mary's home, except for a short spell in London, until her death in 1927. It's still there today, though much altered and extended.

Mary Webb's most famous novels are 'Precious Bane' and 'The Golden Arrow', both of which are imbued with a rich and atmospheric sense of the local landscape. But fame was not forthcoming in Mary's lifetime; sadly, it was only after her death that public acclaim was granted to her, sparked off by posthumous praise from the Prime Minister, Stanley Baldwin. For a few years her books were in demand but they are not popular today, and are all too easy to make fun of (Stella Gibbons's classic 'Cold Comfort Farm' was actually a parody of one of Mary's novels, 'The House in Dormer Forest', written at Spring Cottage). Yet few writers have been as much in tune with their surroundings and anybody who loves Shropshire is likely to enjoy her work.

As it traverses Lyth Hill, the Shropshire Way makes use of what was once a turnpike road from Shrewsbury to the Strettons and Ludlow, which ran through Meole Brace and Bayston Hill then over Lyth Hill, and on through Exfords Green to Stapleton, before joining what is now the A49 at Wayford Bridge, north of Dorrington. It was 'disturnpiked as useless' in 1821, after 70 years of use.

The on-going track leads from the high point of Lyth Hill as a broad track. When it begins to descend you pass the remains of an old windmill, at Windmill House. At a couple of cottages on the edge of Spring Coppice, keep left and go forward through a gate and on through stands of broom. The on-going track descends across open hill pasture. The view to the left is one of rolling, undulating farmlands that characterise much of the Shropshire Way.

The path comes down to meet a stony track at a bend. Go forward down this to a lane. Turn left for 100m/yds and then leave the lane, on the right, just before a road junction, turning right onto another stony track between mature hedgerows. When the track forks, branch right and continue to a stile beside an old Primitive Methodist Chapel (1831), now used for storage. Cross a stile and go in front of the chapel to another stile, and over this bear left down the left-hand edge of the ensuing field.

At the bottom of the field cross another stile, turn right and walk out to a lane at Lower Common. Turn right along the lane until you can turn left at The Hollies on a track to Vinnals. When you reach Vinnals, go through the farmyard and bear right on a dirt track down between hedgerows. The track brings you down to a ford with a not-so-obvious footbridge concealed in undergrowth on the right. Over this continue on a hedgeway (a hedged green lane). Eventually the on-going path through the old green lane takes you left through a hedgerow. Turn right then walk along the right-hand margin of an arable field.

Further on the track dips back into the leafy cover of the green lane and continues as before. When the green lane comes out to meet a farm track continue forward over a stile into an arable field. Go across the ensuing field to the far corner where a stile gives access to a lane. Cross the lane and a stile opposite, and then go forward along the right-hand field edge to a footbridge. Continue in the same direction across the next field, following the course of a brook. When you reach a lane, cross it, and turn right for a few strides to a stile. Beyond, walk forward alongside a post and wire fence.

At the far side of the field cross a brook by a concrete footbridge. Go forward in the same direction across the next pasture to a fence gap on the other side, to the right of a metal gate. Continue along the edge of an arable field, following the field margin around until you reach a footbridge. Beyond this cross the next field to reach a lane, close by Cottage Farm. Turn right along the lane and follow it for a little over 2kms (1 mile) past Wilderley Lane Farm and on to Wilderley Hall Farm. As you reach the farm turn left onto a rising stony track opposite.

Wilderley is just a scattering of farms and cottages, buried deep in this remote country north-west of the Long Mynd. Wilderley Hall has a long pedigree but has been modernised out of all recognition and is obscured by farm buildings. Shortly after you join the stony track, the scant remains of a Norman motte and bailey castle are visible in a neighbouring clump of trees.

When the track turns into a field, keep forward on a green track, through a gate, and on beyond on a wider green track that rises through gorse to the bottom edge of a large sloping pasture. Go up the left edge of the pasture, and at the top cross a stile, a farm access and another stile, and go forward in the next field with a hedgerow on your left. Ignore a stile on your left, but keep forward instead to the left of a slight mound, and go on to reach a metal gate. Beyond the gate go up the next field edge. At the top take the stile to the left of a gate, and continue up the ensuing pasture on a broad grassy track.

As you gain height so the view improves of the rolling Shropshire hillsides to the west, extending into the Welsh border hills, and including the first glimpse of Stiperstones.

When you reach a high point level with the south-westerly corner of a plantation, keep on in much the same direction across the grassy expanse of Wilderley Hill to find a couple of stiles in distant fences. Beyond these go across to a solitary boundary stone with the inscription, 'Manor of Cothercot T J Powys 1791'.

From the stone turn left to a gate about 50m/yds distant, cross a

Shrewsbury Castle
Corndon from Stiperstones

Bull Street and coat of arms, Bishop's Castle
Clun Castle

stile and go forward onto a broad track, the Portway.

The Portway is an ancient road which runs along the top of the Long Mynd. Though much of it has been metalled, it provides a superb walk, with wonderful views all the way. It has been in use for at least 4,000 years and there are more than forty prehistoric tumuli beside it or close to it, while the occasional stone tool has also been found. It was probably a trade route, as its name implies – port means 'market' – and the southern section of it may later have been used by drovers coming from mid-Wales by way of the Kerry Ridgeway, Bishop's Castle and Plowden.

As you walk along the Portway you get a better view to the west of Stiperstones, and to the east an occasional glimpse of the Stretton Hills. Follow the Portway towards the top of Betchcott Hill until a gate bars further progress. Just before this, turn right, over a stile, and descend into the grassy maw of the Golden Valley. On reaching a signpost, turn right and cross a brook, and then walk along the course of an old hedgerow to another stile, leading onto a rutted track bound for Lower Darnford Farm.

When you pass through a gate just above the farm, turn right to a gate and stile. Follow the on-going track across a hill pasture. Cross another stile and then keep on in the same direction, passing a small group of beech trees before continuing along a grassy course through bracken. An obvious path takes you across a brook and then on along a terraced path leading down to a ford and bridge on the edge of Ratlinghope (locally pronounced Ratchup).

[Brow Farm at Ratlinghope is open for refreshments at weekends and bank holidays, and also by arrangement for groups. The campsite is open all year.]

Ratlinghope is a tiny hamlet today, but it has a long history, as the remains of prehistoric settlements on Ratlinghope Hill and neighbouring Stitt Hill demonstrate. The one on Stitt Hill, Castle Ring, is described by Mary Webb in 'The Golden Arrow', written when she was living at Pontesbury and used to walk to Ratlinghope (called 'Slepe' in the novel) to take tea with a friend.

Around the year 1200 the manor was acquired by Walter Corbet, an Augustinian canon, probably of Wigmore Abbey, and by 1209 the Wigmore canons had founded a small priory at Ratlinghope. There are few records of the priory but it was the administrative centre of an estate which supplied produce to the abbey at Wigmore. There are no visible remains of the domestic buildings, but there are traces of earthworks in a field by St Margaret's Church, though there's no evidence that this is the priory site. The foundations of the church, which was rebuilt c1788, may be those of the original priory church, as may the lower parts of the walls, but there is considerable doubt about this.

A local legend tells of a ghostly funeral procession said to drive from Ratlinghope up to the Mynd when the moon is high. It may have been inspired by sightings of the wild horses that are said to have roamed the area until the 1960s.

Just before the bridge at Ratlinghope, go over a stile on the right and walk into light woodland cover. Cross a track further on (it leads left into Ratlinghope), and into woodland opposite. Go forward along a path roughly parallel with a brook, and always keeping the brook on your left, passing below a canopy of horse and sweet chestnut, sycamore and beech.

Follow the path out to a road, and turn right to walk down into Bridges.

Peacefully located at the confluence of the River East Onny and the Darnford Brook, on the north-western flanks of the Long Mynd, this tiny hamlet presumably derives its name from the presence of a footbridge over the river and a vehicle bridge over the brook. There is a youth hostel and an attractive pub, the Horseshoe Inn, which probably stands on the site of a much older one, perhaps established to serve medieval travellers in the days when the priory still stood at Ratlinghope.

In Mary Webb's novels, the Long Mynd is thinly disguised as 'Wilderhope', but it derives its real name from 'mynydd', the Welsh word for 'mountain', though it's actually a large undulating plateau cut by steep-sided valleys known locally as batches or hollows. It is one of the most distinctive and individual upland ranges in Britain. Clothed in heather, bilberry (whinberry), bracken and wiry moorland grasses, with a scattering of stunted, contorted hawthorns and the occasional holly or rowan, its 2,223 hectares/5,490 acres constitute Britain's most southerly grouse moor, while the sky above is patrolled by raven, buzzard and kestrel. Other moorland birds that occur here include curlew, wheatear, whinchat and ring ouzel. The woodlands in the lower valleys attract the pied flycatcher and tree pipit, while dipper and grey wagtail frequent the fast-flowing streams. It's the largest 'wilderness' area in the Midlands and most of it is common land, owned by the National Trust, ensuring that public access is freely available. The summit, Pole Bank, at 516m/1,695ft,

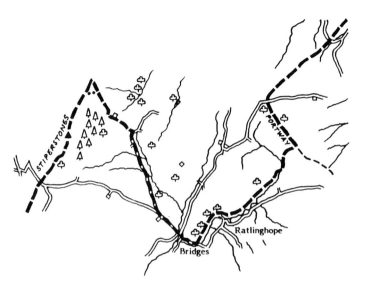

affords spectacular views extending from Snowdonia to the Cotswolds. The Long Mynd has been subject to human use and, to a certain extent, human occupation, since the earliest times. It's liberally dotted with prehistoric remains, including Bronze Age tumuli and an Iron Age fort on Bodbury Hill. By the Middle Ages parts of the Mynd had already become sheepwalk and this pattern of land use still persists. Farmers in surrounding villages retain rights of common, enabling them to graze sheep and ponies on the hill.

To the east of the Long Mynd, on the other side of Church Stretton, rise the Stretton Hills which, like the Wrekin further north, are of volcanic origin. Caer Caradoc, the highest (459m/1,506ft) and shapeliest, is crowned by an impressive hill-fort, and there are a number of lesser prehistoric sites, including the scant remains of two settlements on the Lawley. A mixture of rights of way and concessionary access means that there are endless fine walks available in these superb hills.

BRIDGES TO BISHOP'S CASTLE
Distance: 18.5km (11½ miles)

Between Bridges and Bishop's Castle the only opportunity to obtain refreshments is at Lydham, where there is an excellent and well-stocked wholefood shop and tourist information point. The shop (Harvest Wholefoods) is open Monday-Saturday, 0900-1730.

> *In valleys of springs of rivers,*
> *By Ony and Teme and Clun,*
> *The country for easy livers,*
> *The quietest under the sun.*

In Bridges walk up to a T-junction and turn left. A short way on, turn right on a rising lane (signposted for The Bog and Squilver). Follow the road, hedged by hawthorn, up past Stedment, just beyond which branch right and continue climbing easily. At the top of the lane, where it makes a pronounced right bend, leave it by branching left on a track leading to The Hollies Farm.

Go through The Hollies and onto a rising stony track, shortly bearing right at a signpost. When the track forks 40m/yds later, branch left and ascend to a gate. Keep on up the rutted track beyond to a top gate, where you enter Stiperstones National Nature Reserve.

Stiperstones comprises a long ridge bisected by a lane. The southern half has been tamed, and is mostly forested, but the northern section is rugged heather moorland with a jagged crest of quartzite pinnacles. This extraordinary landscape has its origins in the last Ice Age, when the ridge stood out above the surrounding glaciers and was subjected to intense frost shattering, a process which intensified as the ice slowly began to retreat. The constant freezing and thawing shattered much of the quartzite into a mass of scree surrounding a number of residual tors. Subsequent soil formation has been so slow that much of the scree around the tors remains on the surface, largely unvegetated, giving rough walking. Where soil did form, it was thin, acid and poor in nutrients, but sufficient to support a limited range of acid-tolerant plants. Over most of the moorland summit the vegetation is dominated by heather and bilberry (whinberry), with some crowberry and cowberry (known locally, and incorrectly, as cranberry). Other areas are dominated by the sort of tough, wiry grasses which flourish in acid soils and the limited flora includes bog cotton, cow wheat, heath bedstraw and the occasional mountain pansy. The fauna is also sparse, though meadow pipit, stonechat, curlew, grouse, kestrel, raven and buzzard may be seen.

Stiperstones is rich in minerals, of which lead sulphide was most valuable, though zinc sulphide and barytes have also been mined. It was the Romans who first exploited it and pigs of lead bearing the stamp of Emperor Hadrian have been found. After the Romans departed activity was intermittent until the late eighteenth century when mineral exploitation increased rapidly. For a short time the small, mineral-rich area just to the west of Stiperstones was producing ten per cent of Britain's lead ore.

Stiperstones looms large in Mary Webb's novel 'The Golden Arrow', in which it is known as 'Diafol'. She knew the area intimately and conveys its every mood. D H Lawrence paid only a fleeting visit but was nonetheless inspired to use Stiperstones as a vital element in his novel 'St Mawr' (1925), the central scene of which takes place below the Devil's Chair. Stiperstones (along with other Shropshire locations) also featured in the novels of the popular children's author Malcolm Saville (1901-1982), best known for his Lone Pine adventure stories, nearly all set in the Shropshire hills. For D H Lawrence, Stiperstones was a place where the spirit of 'aboriginal England' could still be felt, and it certainly has the sort of powerful presence that attracts myths and legends. Many of them concern Wild Edric, the Saxon nobleman who briefly resisted the Normans before capitulating in 1070.

One story (which has many variations) tells how Edric was lost one stormy night on Stiperstones and came upon a house filled with beautiful women. Bewitched by their music, he fell in love with one and bore her away to marry her. She warned him that she would often be absent from home but on no account must he question this. Inevitably, the day came when he did, and she vanished for ever, leaving Edric to die of a broken heart. He is said to haunt Stiperstones still. Another story claims that, as punishment for giving up the fight against the invaders, he and his followers were doomed to live eternally in the lead mines beneath Stiperstones, emerging only when England was in danger, when they would ride forth to tackle the enemy. Miners used to claim that they sometimes heard the prisoners knocking underground and whenever this occurred a rich vein of ore would be found.

Modern agriculture has encroached on Stiperstones to a frightening *extent, fragmenting it with areas of 'improved' grassland and conifers so that the ridge no longer turns uniformly purple in August. Fortunately, it has recently been selected for a project christened: 'Back to purple: conserving and restoring the Stiperstones'. This is a Lottery-funded initiative managed by a partnership of English Nature, Forest Enterprise and Shropshire Wildlife Trust. The idea is to convert Forest Enterprise clear-felled land to heath, building on work already carried out over the last decade and part of a long-term effort to restore the highly fragmented heathland ridge to the continuous run of purple it once was. Work will also be done on footpath restoration and provision of disabled access. Some funds are being made available to record local people's memories of, and feelings about, Stiperstones. This is just one of a number of similar heathland restoration projects which Lottery Fund money should shortly be financing throughout the UK.*

Beyond the gate bear right on a track, heading towards the outcrop of Shepherd's Rock. Keep on to a cairn at a track junction, and turn left along the main ridge of Stiperstones. At a cross-track – which can also be reached by a shorter route ascending left from the boundary of the nature reserve – keep on to a prominent rocky cockscomb, known as the Devil's Chair, the summit of which is attainable by easy scrambling.

All sorts of myths and legends swirl around the Devil's Chair. One of them seeks to explain how it got its name: the Devil was carrying an apronful of stones for some evil purpose (it varies, but one version has him planning to dam the Severn and flood Shrewsbury) but spilt them here when he stopped for a rest. Another story has him believing that if only Stiperstones could be made to sink below the earth's surface, all the God-fearing, Bible-reading folk would perish, and so he tries to weigh it down with stones. He and his cronies are said to gather at the Chair on dark nights, while witches congregate at Manstone Rock on the longest night each year to elect a new leader. It is also said that if a human being sits in the Devil's Chair a thunderstorm will at once arise.

After the Devil's Chair you meet Manstone Rock, at 536m/ 1,762ft, the highest point of the ridge, crowned by a trig pillar: this, too, can be 'conquered' by a little scrambling.

Beyond Manstone Rock lies another rocky tor, and shortly after this the most obvious track bears off to the left, heading away from Cranberry Rock, the final outcrop on this part of the ridge. The Way, however, leaves the ridge track between two large,

Cranberry Rock, Stiperstones

collapsed cairns, on a path that heads for Cranberry Rock, and then passes to its right, uncertainly and rockily at first, before improving to a clear path through heather.

The path descends to a track junction close by a wide spread of gorse. Bear right here, in the direction of a lower wooded hillside, the southern extension of the Stiperstones ridge. Follow the path down to a stile/gate, and then to a road. Cross the road, and in the next pasture walk forward along the line of an ancient hedgerow, of which only isolated birches, rowan and a single hawthorn remain.

This guides you to a stile on the edge of a plantation. Beyond this, follow a path deeper into the trees, crossing a wide forest trail, and continuing onto a gently rising pathway opposite. The path soon begins to descend gently through pine trees, and crosses a cleared area before returning to the company of pines. Near a prominent outcrop, where, according to some authorities, a real Rock House is thought to have stood, the path reaches a junction. Turn left here and descend to pass the reputed site of Rock House. The on-going track soon descends more steeply to meet a rough-

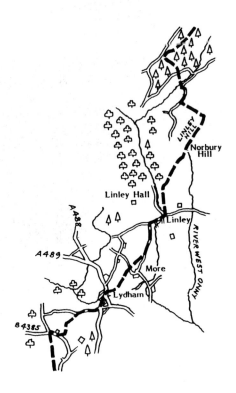

surfaced lane. Turn right for a few strides and then cross a stile. Descend the next field to a footbridge at the bottom.

After the footbridge climb steeply through light woodland to a lane. Turn right along the lane, heading for Ridge Farm, an isolated farmhouse completely surrounded by rolling hillsides. About 150m/yds past the entrance to Ridge Farm leave the lane, going left through the second of two gates. Climb the steep pasture beyond, aiming for a single ash tree on the skyline above. After the tree keep on in the same direction to a stile on the edge of a small plantation. Over this, go forward along the plantation boundary and then by a fence, until you meet a stile and gate.

Cross the stile, and ascend slightly left on a green track that rises beside ancient beeches and a sunken trackway.

Beyond the next gate and stile, the trackway takes you up slightly onto Linley Hill (the highest point of which is known as Norbury Hill), with an improving view to the west of Black Rhadley Hill and Corndon Hill. The track continues to follow the line of beech trees, with many more beeches yet to come, but for the moment they end, near another metal gate. From the gate go forward towards a group of trees in a dip to the left of a low hill.

One of the most popular fashions among landowners in the eighteenth century was the planting of so-called ornamental (that is, non-native) trees in grandiose landscaping schemes. Beech is a native tree, but only in the southern counties of England, and was often used in such schemes. The fine beech avenue on Linley Hill is of uncertain origin. It is shown on a map of 1808, yet tradition suggests that it was planted after the Napoleonic Wars (1803-15), probably by unemployed ex-soldiers. Perhaps the truth is that the post-war planting supplemented, or replaced, an earlier avenue. Some of the older trees are dying now, but later plantings have helped maintain something of the grandeur of this historic and striking feature.

Cross a stile beside a gate at the top end of the beech avenue. As you descend through the trees, the view to the east is particularly inviting, embracing as it does the whaleback of the Long Mynd, its flanks descending into the pattern of green fields that flows across the low-lying hillsides surrounding Bishop's Castle ahead.

Lower down, the descending track runs along the edge of Hayes Wood to a surfaced lane. Turn left down the lane to a T-junction, and turn right. Not far from Linley Hall, cross a small bridge spanning the River West Onny.

Linley Hall is a Palladian mansion designed in 1742 by London architect Henry Joynes, and was the first of its type to be built in Shropshire. Erected on the site of an earlier house, it remains, outwardly at least, very little altered since the eighteenth century. Until a few years ago it belonged to a family who came over with the Conqueror and were rewarded with the manor of More, from which they took their name. One eighteenth-century member of the family, Robert More, was a great traveller and botanist who brought home exotic tree species. He is credited with having planted England's first larch trees in 1783 in the grounds of the hall, where they still stand today, in a sheltered location by a tributary of the River West Onny. The Mores are one of Shropshire's oldest families, but they were not the first people to live at Linley. The site of what appears to have been a Romano-British village has been discovered by the West Onny, close to the point at which the long, tree-lined avenue which leads to Linley Hall joins the road you are walking along. The Romans are known to have mined lead in the hills behind the house and traces of a furnace where lead was processed have been found, together with the remains of an aqueduct.

Directly opposite the front of Linley Hall, turn left down another lane bound for the village of More. Follow the lane until you can leave it, on the right, over a stile in a splendid mixed hedgerow containing hazel, holly, oak, and field maple.

[Walkers wanting to visit More should simply keep on down the lane.]

The village is small and, in many ways, one of the most attractive in the county, with beautiful timber-framed houses clustering round thirteenth-century St Peter's Church, which occupies a circular raised churchyard with huge stones in its enclosing wall, suggesting this was a pre-Christian religious site. The More chapel on the north side of the church was added in the seventeenth century but was substantially rebuilt, along with much of the rest, in 1845. The squat, sturdy, Norman tower has a stepped pyramid top similar to more famous examples at Clun and Hopesay.

After crossing the stile go half-left across the ensuing field to a stile in the middle of a fence, and then cross a small enclosed pasture to another stile. Beyond that, head towards the most distant of three pylons. This will steer you to a small metal gate giving onto a lane.

Cross the lane and go over a stile, continuing beyond on an indistinct green path bearing left. Just as the on-going path passes beneath the power line, close by an oak and an ash, continue by following the route of the power lines. For a while you appear to be walking along an overgrown causeway that may have served in the past as a church road, or, more likely, was part of a street in the medieval village that stood on this site.

The Shropshire Way here passes through the site of a Norman motte and bailey castle, marked only by a series of earthworks. The castle would have been built of timber and raised on a motte, which survives as a low mound defended by ditches. Just to the east of it are two large rectangular baileys (outer enclosures), while a number of other earthworks may be house platforms, indicating that the village has either moved or shrunk since the Middle Ages. The site is known to local people as the Moatlands.

The causeway leads to a stile and footbridge over a brook, beyond which you go diagonally left across a field, heading for an isolated oak tree in mid-field. Keep on beyond that to a stile in a field corner. Go half-left across the next field, heading for the just visible roof of a building, and this will guide you to a stile at the rear of buildings at Lydham. Beyond the stile walk out to the main road and turn left, immediately bearing right along the road for Bishop's Castle (A488).

It may seem unlikely, but in the Anglo-Saxon era Lydham was regarded as a town. Like many such, it never realised its potential and is now just an unremarkable village strung out along the main road. The village centre is grouped around Holy Trinity Church, which was built in the thirteenth century but substantially restored in 1642 and again in 1885. Behind the church is the mound of a Norman motte and bailey castle. Just to the south of the village, and bypassed by the Shropshire Way, is Lydham Manor, surrounded by (private) parkland which contains a number of very fine trees, including the Lydham Oak, one of the largest oaks in the country.

Walk down the A488 for about 300m/yds, and then leave it, on the right, at a signposted path heading along a broad gravel track between hedgerows. When the track bends to the right leave it, on the left, over a stile beside double gates. Go half-left across the next field to a distant gate and stile. Enter the next field and follow the right-hand field margin round until just past a gate you draw level with an old oak tree on the left.

Lydham Manor with its famous trees is also to your left at this point. Go right here, through a dip, into the next field. Cross this to the far left corner, where a stile gives onto the B4385 at the entrance to Upper Heblands Farm. Turn right onto the road until, just opposite the turning to Churchstoke, you can leave it, over a stile on the left.

At this point in the walk you are at one of the closest points along the main route to the Anglo-Welsh border, and many of the hills that lie a short distance away – Corndon, Lan Fawr and Roundton – are in Wales.

Go up the ensuing field, initially alongside a hedgerow and then beside the edge of a plantation. At the top edge of the plantation keep on in the same direction to a stile in a hedge corner. Beyond this go along the left-hand field edge to another stile, beside a sycamore tree. Go on a few strides to cross another fence and hedgerow, and then head down to the left of some corrugated iron barns. Nearby, cross into the next field, and ascend half-left, heading for a black and white cottage beside which a stile in a corner gives onto a passageway between houses. Turn right at the road just ahead (Castle Green), and follow it round and down to the top of Bull Street.

Turn right into Bull Street, and keep forward to High Street and the centre of Bishop's Castle.

BISHOP'S CASTLE TO CLUN
Distance: 17.5km (11 miles)

From Bishop's Castle to Clun there is no scope for taking refreshment along the way, so be sure to go adequately supplied.

Bishop's Castle

The documented history of Bishop's Castle begins in the late eighth century when it was part of the manor of Lydbury North, whose Saxon lord, Egwin Shakehead, gave it to the Bishop of Hereford after he had been cured of the palsy at the tomb of St Ethelbert in Hereford Cathedral. The castle was built about 1127 by another Bishop of Hereford on a site at the top of the present town, behind Castle Hotel. It was kept in good repair throughout the Middle Ages and into the Tudor period but became ruinous in the early seventeenth century. What little survives can be visited from Castle Street. The Castle Hotel lies in the middle of the outer bailey and a path from the back of the hotel leads to the top of the motte, which is now a bowling green.

The little town may have lost its castle, but it retains many other reminders of its long history, with a harmonious mix of architecturally diverse buildings. Most are simply pleasing and appropriate, rather than notable, but some, such as the Castle Hotel and the Porch House, are architecturally distinguished. The High Street rises steeply and narrows at the top, by the tiny eighteenth-century Town Hall. Next to it is the House on Crutches, an Elizabethan building with its gable end supported on wooden posts, and the view from here, to not-so-distant green hills, is an enticing one.

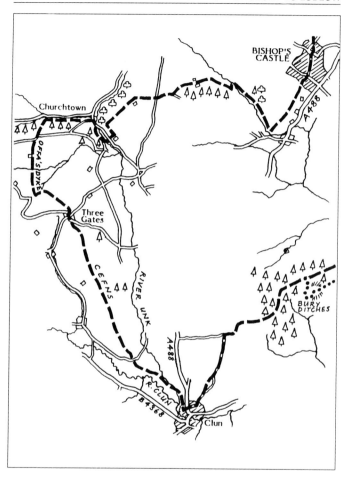

In the early Middle Ages the parish of Bishop's Castle was partly in England, partly in Wales, and often the subject of dispute. It was always a significant Marches' township with people from both sides of the border making good use of its markets. It received its first charter in 1278, but in 1573 Queen Elizabeth I granted a new charter and from 1585 Bishop's Castle returned two MPs to Westminster. At one time it was the smallest borough in England, known as a 'rotten borough' (one of

The Poppy House, Market Square, Bishop's Castle

many) because its small population didn't justify two MPs. Even worse, in 1820, all four candidates polled 87 votes each and in the absence of any other procedure all were duly elected. The Reform Act of 1832 put an end to this sort of thing and also to Bishop's Castle's political significance, though it remained a borough until 1967.

The Castle, as locals call it, was once a railway town too, at the end of a line built in 1865 from Craven Arms and usually described as 'eccentric' or 'bizarre' because it never had a chance of making a profit. Immensely scenic, the route was never financially viable and closed in 1935, though it is remembered affectionately at the town's Railway Museum.

Bishop's Castle is also known for its real ale. The Three Tuns is a historic brew pub which obtained its licence in 1642, though the present brewhouse is Victorian. The Six Bells, a seventeenth-century coaching inn, also offers beer brewed on site.

Though the prevailing impression is often of a sleepy sort of place this is not altogether accurate. Friday is a good day to be in Bishop's Castle, when a colourful and lively market takes over the Town Hall, and there is plenty going on throughout the year, from a May Fair to a Christmas lights festival in December. Morris dancing, a rush-bearing ceremony, a carnival, a real ale festival and a steam fair all feature in the annual *calendar of events. Above all, Bishop's Castle has immense charm and character and it really is worth taking the time to explore it properly.*

The church is dedicated to St John the Baptist, and though a church is known to have existed on this site in 1291, little remains from this time, though the characteristically sturdy border tower may be the original Norman one. St John's was fortified in the Civil War, probably as a refuge for local people, but possibly for use by the Parliamentarians, and was burned down in retaliation by the Royalists in 1644. It was subsequently rebuilt but then rebuilt again in 1860.

Walk down the main street towards the church, turn right at the Six Bells pub, and then go immediately left into Church Lane. When you reach the turning for Field Lane, branch right, and 20m/yds later, left, up a hedgeway.

Go past Field Cottage and keep forward over a stile beside a gate, and then on along a green trackway to a junction with another farm track. Go through a gate and start descending slightly. Keep forward to a gate and stile where the main track bears left down through a gate, and leave it at this point to continue alongside a hedgerow along the bottom of a field. Cross the bottom edge of a second field to a stile, and then continue beside a hawthorn and holly hedgerow. From a hedge corner go forward towards a vehicle track and gate a short distance ahead. When you intercept a track coming from the gate, turn right to go past an old quarry, and then along a narrow sheep trod, roughly parallel with a tree-lined brook about 40m/yds to the left.

In the next pasture keep on in the same direction, and repeat this across a number of fields, never far from the brook. In places the field margins can be muddy after wet weather. Eventually you reach Woodbatch Lane at a gate. Turn left, and after about 100m/yds bend right, rising gently.

The banks of the lane in spring host a wide range of flowers including red campion, stitchwort, foxglove, yellow archangel – an indicator of ancient woodland, especially when, as here, it is found in association with bluebell and dog's mercury – honeysuckle, lesser celandine, vetch and wild strawberry. In parts the hedgerow is traditionally laid. The glory of the hedgerow, sadly, does not continue up to Middle Woodbatch Farm, where electric fencing, rubbish and scrap cars seem to be preferred.

Keep ascending past the farm. Beyond its buildings, when the rising track forks, branch left and ascend a holloway. Keep climbing, with the open woodland of Henley Wood on your left. When you reach its top edge, go forward, still on a holloway. About 130m/yds further on, at a post and wire fence, turn left alongside it. At the top of the field, turn right for a short distance to a stile beside a gate. Beyond this turn right and walk beside a fence and intermittent hedgerow along a field margin.

The track runs out to meet a lane at Reilthtop, near Vron Farm. Turn left along the lane for 50m/yds, and then leave it, on the right, at a metal gate. Go to another gate a few strides further on, and then pursue a beautiful, broad, grassy track flanked by hawthorn, ash and holly, that may well have been an old drove road.

When the track bends left, go with it, and start descending gently. The track runs down to a gate at the top edge of a large sloping field. Ignore the tempting vehicle track curving left down-field, but go forward on a broad grassy track beside a hedge. At the far side of the field you meet a sunken trackway, descending left. Go down this.

At the bottom, having rejoined the earlier track, turn right

Between Bishop's Castle and Mainstone

through a metal gate and go down a hedgeway to meet a road.

Cross the road and go forward down the lane opposite. Just after crossing the River Unk, leave the lane, on the right, through a small forestry compound, and onto a forest track.

From here to the summit of Cefns, the Shropshire Way undulates considerably, notably as it associates with Offa's Dyke Path, which is sampled for a while.

As the forest track starts a pronounced rise, look for a stile on the edge of the plantation, just to the right and down a short path. Beyond this go down to another stile and then left across the ensuing field to a stile giving onto a surfaced lane. Turn left along this and then 20m/yds later, turn left at Cow Pasture Gate onto another lane. Go up the lane for a few minutes until you can leave it, on the right, at a gate and stile, and go forward on a track through light woodland, descending initially, and then levelling as it goes forward to a stile on the edge of Churchtown Wood. Over the stile, keep forward along a path at the bottom edge of the wood.

Sheltering deep in Cwm Ffrydd below is the tiny hamlet of Churchtown, behind which Offa's Dyke and its accompanying path can be seen ascending the hillside.

Offa was ruler of the dominant English kingdom of Mercia between 757 and 796, and the dyke that bears his name is the longest archaeological monument in Britain, an enormously impressive structure that stretched originally from Prestatyn to Chepstow along the border between England and Wales. Of the original 240kms (150 miles), a total of 128kms (80 miles) of earthworks are still visible, consisting mainly of a bank, with a ditch on the Welsh side. Nobody is certain why Offa ordered its construction – possibly for defensive purposes, maybe just to define the border or to act as a sort of customs barrier to assist in the regulation of cross-border trade. Offa's Dyke National Trail, opened in 1971, is a splendid walk that follows the dyke for much of its length but deviates from it in places.

With just a couple of cottages keeping the church company, Churchtown is actually part of Mainstone, a slightly larger hamlet some distance away. The church, dedicated to St John the Baptist and also known as the Church on the Dyke, is Mainstone's parish church. The explanation for this confusing situation may be that the main settlement was once at Churchtown, which was larger than it is today, and for some unknown reason the centre of population moved down the valley to the east. The name Mainstone is derived from the Welsh 'maen' meaning 'stone' (i.e. 'stone-stone') and the stone in question is supposedly the smooth granite boulder that now sits inside St John's at Churchtown, on the floor beside the pulpit. What it is doing there nobody knows, though there is a tangle of legends surrounding it. The church was restored in 1887 but some older features were preserved, notably a magnificent Elizabethan oak roof.

The woodland path ends at a stile, beyond which you descend for a few strides to join Offa's Dyke Path. Turn left, and climb back up into woodland on a steeply rising path that leads to a stile. Beyond this, keep on in the same direction, still following Offa's Dyke, and walking along a ditch between raised embankments flanked by hawthorn, to a stile at a surfaced lane. Over the stile turn right and 10m/yds later leave the lane, on the left. Walk to another stile, beyond which you descend beside Offa's Dyke, which is capped by a fence and a hawthorn hedgerow. Go down to cross a brook, and climb again beyond that to meet the access to Middle Knuck, now the Corvedale Care Centre.

Cross the centre's access to a stile and then go left past a corrugated iron barn to another stile, beyond which you descend once more, using the ditch that runs alongside the dyke. Go down steeply to the foot of a pasture to cross a brook by a footbridge. On the other side, climb on a path along the left field edge, and beside some well-established sycamore trees, and later walk alongside a fence and the on-going dyke, in the company of hawthorn and hazel trees.

When the path crosses to the other side of the fence along the top of the dyke then your time spent in the company of Offa's Dyke Path is coming to an end. Go down to another stile and then forward to a waymark. Bear right to a signpost about 30m/yds before a gate and a surfaced lane, and leave Offa's Dyke Path by turning sharp left onto a rising track. It goes past an old quarry and then forward across the large open pastures of Hergan with fine views off to the left of rolling pastures and the not-so-distant border hills of Wales.

On the far side of the pasture cross a stile by a gate and go down the ensuing field. In the next field keep on in the same direction, with Three Gates Farm eventually coming into view, behind which the swelling ridge of Cefns looms, while away to the right lies the Clun valley. The on-going path descends into a holloway flanked by hawthorns, and takes you down to a road at Three Gates. Turn left and go past two side roads, left and right, then keep forward until, just after the last farm buildings, at a bend, you can leave the on-going lane by branching right through the right-hand of two gates onto a rising track.

Keep on the track through two more gates and then follow a fence and hedgerow on your right to another stile, beyond which cross the sloping pasture ahead to the high point of Cefns ridge. From here go forward with a fenceline and an intermittent row of hawthorns.

As you descend this superb ridge the landscape that unfolds all around is one of rolling patterned hillsides and lush green valleys. The long descent is delicious leg-swinging freedom, striding forward into the folds of the verdant Shropshire countryside surrounding the town of Clun.

The descending ridge path gradually becomes more pronounced as it runs on to meet a stile at the head of an old trackway which in spring and summer is brightly coloured with foxgloves in great number, as well as stitchwort, broom and red campion.

When the descending track reaches a stile beside a gate, cross it and in so doing acquire a hedgerow and fence on your right-hand side. Keep on to another gate and stile, and maintain the same direction across a field to a signpost, and then go down beside a fence on your right to a concealed stile. After this descend the next field, following its right-hand margin to a stile giving onto a road.

Turn right for a few strides, and then go left over a stile beside a metal gate onto a hedged green lane. The on-going path is clear, waymarked where needed, and leads to an enclosed pathway descending to the River Unk. Cross a stile by the river and go left, then at a footbridge go left into the next field. With Clun Castle coming into view ahead, follow the left-hand field edge, walking parallel with the river until you can cross it by a footbridge. Turn right and walk along a hedged green lane beside the river towards Clun. Pass some cottages, where the lane becomes rough-surfaced. When it bends left, leave it, going ahead over a stile, and a few strides later turn right through a gate, and immediately left on a path alongside an intermittent hedgerow leading up to a gate and stile at the entrance to Clun Castle.

Through the stile turn left and walk down past cottages to the junction with Enfield Street and Church Street.

Clun

Clun is set in the most beautiful countryside. Enfolded by enticing green hills on all sides, its grey houses slumber beside church and castle close to the confluence of the lovely River Clun with its tributary, the Unk. The surrounding area has a long history of human occupation, with Stone Age people known to have been present at least 5,000 years ago. Later, from around 1500BC, an important Bronze Age trade route ran from Anchor, on the present Welsh border, across Clun Forest and the Clee Hills to cross the Severn at Bewdley, and although its exact route can no longer be traced in full it is known as the Clun-Clee Ridgeway.

Clun itself may have been settled as early as the Bronze Age. There are two parts to the town (and it is a town, even if it appears to be a village), with the original settlement based around the church just to the south of the river. The roughly circular churchyard is an indication that the site may have had pre-Christian religious significance, and there may later have been a Celtic church here.

The name Clun is a Celtic one, related to the Welsh 'llan', which means 'sacred place' or 'church'. There is known to have been an Anglo-Saxon church, and at least one of the yews in the churchyard dates from that time – it is well over 1,000 years old and possibly the oldest in the county. The present church, dedicated to St George, was built by the Normans but was restored in 1877, using much of the original stone. The sturdy, square, twelfth-century tower, topped with a truncated pyramidal roof, is characteristic of border churches and probably served as a place of refuge from raiders. Parliamentary soldiers occupied the church in the Civil War, when it was partly burnt in a Royalist attack (the people of Clun formed an association, the Clubman's Society, to defend their town against both Roundheads and Royalists).

Across the fourteenth-century bridge is the 'new town', itself 900 years old, and laid out by the Normans in a regular grid pattern which still survives. On its western edge are the ruins of their castle, built by Robert (better known as Picot) de Say in c1099, and obviously intended to dominate the surrounding countryside. It was rebuilt in stone in 1140, and later passed by marriage to the FitzAlans, and then, in the early sixteenth century, to Thomas Howard, Duke of Norfolk. It was besieged and damaged on several occasions, once by King John, another time by Prince Llewelyn, again by Owain Glyndwr, but became largely redundant after peace came to the Marches, especially as the FitzAlans spent most of their time at their considerably grander home at Arundel.

St George's Church, Clun

Still owned by the Duke of Norfolk, and managed by English Heritage, it's freely accessible to visitors. Apart from the interest of the castle itself, the short climb to the top of the motte reveals tempting views of the surrounding countryside.

Clun was granted its town charter in the fourteenth century, with the right to hold a Saturday market and two annual fairs. For many years it was a bustling place with numerous shops and pubs and a busy livestock market. Decline set in during the nineteenth century when the railways boosted the fortunes of other towns but avoided Clun altogether. At least this meant that it escaped the rapid development which characterised the nineteenth and twentieth centuries, and it remains relatively unspoilt.

As well as the obvious ones, such as church and castle, Clun is full of interesting buildings, including Trinity Hospital Almshouses, founded in 1614 by Henry Howard, Earl of Northampton, for twelve poor men, who were summoned to prayer by a bell and subject to a 9pm curfew. Today, the almshouses can accommodate fifteen residents, men and women, under rather less strict conditions. Also worth seeing is the Town Hall, built by Lord Clive in 1780, and now the home of an interesting little museum, but most of Clun's buildings are quietly attractive and it's a pleasure just to wander around its unspoilt streets.

Literary connections abound in Clun. E M Forster, for instance, visited the town, which subsequently featured as Oniton in 'Howard's End'. One of the characters in the book, Margaret Schlegel, is totally captivated by the romance and magic of this corner of the Marches and it's not hard to see why. The castle is said to have been the inspiration for Garde Doleureuse in Sir Walter Scott's novel 'The Betrothed', published in 1825. Scott is believed to have stayed at the Buffalo Inn while working on the book. More recently, playwright John Osborne lived near Clun and now lies buried in the churchyard.

CLUN TO STOKESAY CASTLE (Craven Arms)
Distance: 17.8km (11 miles)

Although the Way between Clun and Stokesay Castle passes through two small villages – Kempton and Hopesay – neither provides refreshments, and walkers should ensure they are adequately equipped in that department before setting off.

Cross into Newport Street opposite, climbing easily past cottages. Continue along the lane, following it round and heading for the youth hostel. Keep on past the hostel, and then, about 100m/yds further on, leave the lane, going left beside a garage just past Lake Cottage, to walk up a waymarked vehicle track to Mill Barn Cottage.

Pass round the cottage on an enclosed pathway to a stile. Strike across a field to another stile, and beyond that keep on in the same direction to pass through a hawthorn hedgerow and then by a curving green path to rejoin the surfaced lane at a stile.

Turn left up the lane to Guilden Down, bear right between farm buildings, and continue to an isolated house on the left. Turn left here on a broad vehicle track, and follow the on-going track as it rises gently to a gate on the edge of Forestry Commission land around Steppleknoll and Sunnyhill. Go forward beyond the gate, climbing to meet a graded forestry track. This section of the walk is also shared with Wild Edric's Way and the Jack Mytton Way.

The Jack Mytton Way, a medium-distance bridleway, was officially opened in 1993. It runs for 114kms/71 miles, from Billingsley in the Severn Valley to Llanfair Waterdine on the Powys border.

The eponymous Jack Mytton was born in 1796 at Halston, near

Oswestry, and is one of the county's most colourful characters. He became MP for Shrewsbury, but found the proceedings of the House of Commons too tedious to detain him for long. In fact, it is said he managed only half an hour before storming out, never to return. He was a drunk and a gambler, given to wild exploits and crazy practical jokes that earned him the nickname 'Mad Jack'. He wasted a huge fortune and died of a stroke in 1834 in a debtors' prison in London.

Turn right along the forest track, and when it forks, branch left, rising slightly. When the track reaches its highest point the Way divides.

The official route goes forward, downhill to the edge of the forest and then across two fields, beside a hedgerow on the right, to reach a lane just south of Lower Down. At the lane turn right for about 400m/yds until you reach the turning for the Bury Ditches hill-fort, where the second route emerges.

This more satisfying route branches right at the high point, following a forest track around the western edge of the fort as far as a stile on the left by means of which Bury Ditches is accessed. After the stile follow an obvious path rising through the ramparts, with an optional diversion left to a splendid viewpoint with a toposcope. Returning to the main path, go down to another stile and gate, and then steadily downward to reach a car park and picnic area.

One of the most formidable of the Shropshire hill-forts, Bury Ditches dates from the first century BC and had two entrances defended by banks and ditches, particularly well-defined on the north side. The view from the top is one of the finest in Shropshire, including Stiperstones and its neighbours, the Long Mynd, Wenlock Edge and the Clee Hills, while the rounded tops of Clun Forest lead the eye towards the Kerry Hills of Powys. This view was lost for several years, after the Forestry Commission planted the top of the fort with fast-growing conifers. Fortunately, an opportune gale in 1978 flattened many of the trees and the Commission took the hint and cleared the rest.

Bury Ditches was not just a fortification but a major centre of permanent settlement, in what was quite densely populated countryside in prehistoric times. Most of the surrounding hills also have ancient settlements on them e.g. Caer Caradoc (at Chapel Lawn, not to be confused with its namesake in the Stretton Hills), Caer-din Ring, Fron Camp, Burrow and others.

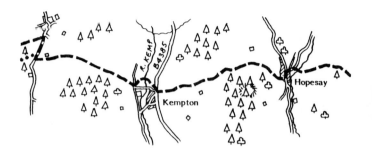

Leave the car park onto the road, turn right and go downhill for about 100m/yds, and then leave the road, on the left, over a stile beside a gate, and go down a vehicle access to Stanley Cottage. Go in front of the cottage and over a stile, going forward onto a track into a dingle. About 400m/yds past Stanley Cottage, leave the on-going track by descending right into mixed woodland on a signposted path that soon parallels the course of a brook. Keep along the path until it emerges on a broad, graded track near Lodge Farm. Go past the farm and forward towards the village of Kempton. When the track forks about 1km (half a mile) later, branch right for about 30m/yds to a step stile over a fence on the left. Immediately cross another stile a few strides later, then the ensuing field, heading for a conspicuous white gate to the right of a cottage on the far side.

Through the gate, go forward on a gravel path to another gate/stile, and then out on an access track for 30m/yds. Leave the track, over a stile on the right, to cross a large meadow, aiming to the right of a white cottage in the distance. The path leads you to a small, gated enclosure. After the second gate, turn left and walk up a concrete track to the main road. Turn right, going past a white cottage, Old Kempton Stores, the former village shop.

Kempton is a tiny place of farms and a few cottages sheltering in the valley of the River Kemp, another tributary of the Clun. It's most notable for Walcot Park, which was one of several properties belonging to Robert Clive (1725-74) who achieved wealth and fame as 'Clive of India'.

Turn left 100m/yds later, leaving the road for the rising access to Barlow House Farm. Just as you reach the high point of the track, leave it, on the right, through a waymarked gate. Bear slightly left in the ensuing field to another gate. Through the gate walk down beside a fenceline on the right to a track junction at a trio of gates. Take the third gate, then head across the next field, aiming for a small group of oak trees.

At the trees, go through another gate and down the next field, gradually bearing right to enter a hedged green lane that leads you down to St Mary's Church in Hopesay.

Tucked away in a secluded valley below steep slopes, Hopesay is a delightfully peaceful place. Sadly, there is said to be nobody of local origin living in the village today, and there is no shop, pub, school or bus service. Many of the older houses are surprisingly large and grand for so small a village, so presumably it has long been seen as a desirable place to live. It seems that several of the smaller houses were originally built for servants.

Hopesay Farmhouse in the village centre is the oldest surviving building, apart from the church, and is a mixture of timber-framing and stone. St Mary's Church is of Norman origin, with a distinctive arched doorway of c1160 and a splendid, chestnut-panelled nave roof which is probably fifteenth-century. The broad, low tower dates from c1200, looks defensive in purpose and is very reminiscent of the one at Clun.

Next to the church members of The Friends of Hopesay Meadow, and other volunteers, have created a small nature reserve, comprising a wildflower meadow, two ponds, a mixed-species hedge, areas of scrub and woodland planted only with trees and shrubs native to south Shropshire and smaller features such as a compost heap and a wood pile, both of which provide valuable habitats as well as helping to demonstrate natural recycling in action. The mixed-species hedge was planted in 1991 with natives such as hawthorn, holly, hazel, field maple and crab apple. The intention is to layer it in the traditional Midlands style once it is growing vigorously enough. The trees were planted by local children and other volunteers and when the trees are old enough (about ten years) coppicing will commence.

Keep on past the church and go down to the main road. Turn left, and shortly leave the road at the first turning on the right (signposted: Round Oak). Walk down the lane for about 200m/yds, and then leave it for another lane on the right heading for Hopesay

Hill. Just after Brookside Cottage, leave the lane, branching right between hedges onto a track rising to a gate.

Hopesay Hill is a glorious expanse of rough brackeny land with marvellous views. Until the early nineteenth century it was, with all the surrounding high ground, common land used as sheepwalk. The land was hedged at the time of the Enclosures, but for some reason Hopesay was not subdivided and it survived as one large open pasture. It was bequeathed to the National Trust in 1952, otherwise it would almost certainly have been ploughed, drained and reseeded. The soil is acid and nutrient-poor, and bracken has rampaged across the hillside, two factors which have resulted in a rather impoverished flora. Nevertheless, the short springy turf is brightened by the vivid yellow flowers of tormentil in the summer. The National Trust lets the hill for grazing, thus maintaining its traditional use, and efforts are being made to limit the spread of the bracken. Birds to be seen here include buzzard, kestrel, wheatear and skylark. The latter is becoming dangerously rare throughout Britain but is still quite common in many parts of Shropshire.

Beyond the gate the path rises a few strides to an oak tree, and then climbs onto the hill through bracken. As you reach the high point of Hopesay Hill, go forward to a gate at the edge of Oldfield Wood. Keep on, with the boundary of Oldfield Wood on your right, and descend to a ruined brick building. Just past the ruin, bear right, still following the woodland edge.

When you reach a gate, head for a couple of oak trees in the next field, then go down beside a hedgerow on the left to the bottom of the field, where there is a concealed stile near a cottage. In spring the lower part of the field is yellow-bright with a carpet of lesser celandine.

Go past the cottage, and then head across the large pasture that follows, aiming for a stile about 150m/yds to the right of Castle Farm at Sibdon Carwood.

A charming and secluded little community, Sibdon Carwood consists of little more than farm, church and a couple of houses.

So-called Sibdon Castle is not a real castle, just a castellated country house. It is believed to have been built in the seventeenth century, modernised in the eighteenth and Gothicised at the beginning of the nineteenth.

St Michael's Church is of 1741 but was Gothicised in 1871 to match the house. It's believed to stand on the site of a twelfth-century building

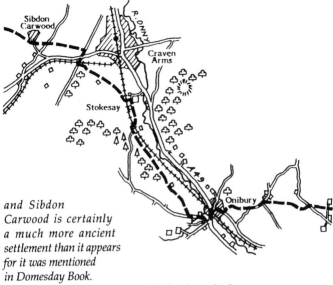

and Sibdon Carwood is certainly a much more ancient settlement than it appears for it was mentioned in Domesday Book.

A small footbridge spans a ditch, after which you cross a narrow field to a kissing gate. Cross an access and go through another gate, and then forward again, gradually bearing left to meet a hedgerow. Follow this to meet a lane. Cross the lane and go over another stile, and in the ensuing field head for the far left corner. Here leave the field, and then turn right, following an on-going hedgerow and then a fence across three fields to meet a lane, where you turn right.

Although not immediately obvious, this is a Roman road, Watling Street. The 'street' ran from Branogenium (now Leintwardine) to Viroconium (now Wroxeter). In places the modern A49 follows its course, but elsewhere it survives as minor roads, bridleways and footpaths. In places it has been lost, but its course can still be traced on the map.

[Walkers bound for Craven Arms should, however, cross the lane and follow a path ahead, which shortly joins the B4368 on the edge of the town. Turn left along this to a road junction, and left again.]

Craven Arms

Craven Arms is an ugly but functional town with a useful range of services. It owes its existence in its present form to the building of the railways, before which it consisted of little more than a hotel by a road junction and a huddle of cottages at the hamlet of Newton, by the River Onny. The hotel, the Craven Arms, stands by the junction of the A49 Hereford-Shrewsbury road and the B4368 which runs east to Much Wenlock and west through the Clun valley to Wales, and was probably used by cattle drovers at one time. Just to the west of Craven Arms is the Romans' Watling Street. It seems likely, from this conjunction of roads, that the present hotel must occupy the site of a much older inn, built to serve the needs of travellers many centuries ago.

In the 1840s the Hereford-Shrewsbury railway was built, closely followed by the Knighton line to Wales, the Buildwas line to the coal-fields and the Bishop's Castle line, making Craven Arms a major railway junction. The cattle and sheep that had travelled the drove roads now came by train and plenty of other transport opportunities were opened up. Local landowner the Earl of Craven recognised the potential for profit and responded by building a new town. For a while it seemed as though it might grow into a major centre but this never happened, though there are still huge livestock sales at The Arms, as locals call it. The best-looking building in town is still the hotel from which it took its name, and opposite this there stands an interesting milestone, in the form of an obelisk, with numerous towns and their distances from Craven Arms inscribed on it. The old hamlet of Newton still exists as a pleasant enclave of cottages at the south-east corner of town.

Follow the lane down to meet and cross the B4368. Keep on along the lane towards Rowton, and pass beneath a railway bridge, and then immediately go left over a stile. Follow the left-hand hedgerow in the next field as far as a hedge junction, and then turn right alongside a rising hedgerow to walk up to a stile in the top corner of the field. Over this enter Sallow Coppice and turn left, leaving the woodland about 100m/yds further on into a large open pasture.

Managed by Forest Enterprise, Sallow Coppice is one of the few remnants of ancient woodland on the southern end of the Wenlock lime-stone escarpment that has not been converted to conifers. It did suffer extensive felling in the 1940s but was allowed to regenerate naturally and there is a fine mix of broad-leaved trees, including oak, birch, wild cherry, sweet chestnut and lime, though there are not large numbers of the eponymous sallow. There is an interesting ground flora, and it is particularly lovely in spring, with primrose, violet, wood anemone, woodruff and ransoms among the species which flourish here.

Go left and down the edges of two fields, finally being deflected right to go under another railway line. Then go forward through a gate to walk beside a pond towards the rear of Stokesay Castle.

Stokesay Castle

Not really a castle at all, but a fortified manorhouse, the almost impossibly picturesque Stokesay Castle nestles in lovely countryside next to a timber-framed Elizabethan gatehouse and the parish church. It is the best-preserved and probably the oldest example of its kind in England.

The manor of Stoke was originally held by the de Say family, but in 1280 it was sold to a wealthy wool merchant, Laurence of Ludlow, who set about rebuilding and fortifying the house, once he had obtained a 'licence to crenellate' from Edward I. However, the architectural style owes more to fashion than to any real need for fortification, and Stokesay could not have resisted prolonged assault.

The Tudor Gatehouse at Stokesay Castle

61

Ten generations of Laurence's descendants lived at Stokesay but in the reign of Charles I it came into the ownership of the Craven family and was used as a supply base for the King's forces when they were based at Ludlow in the early stages of the Civil War. It was surrendered to the Roundheads without a siege when it came under attack. By the nineteenth century it had fallen into decay, and was being used as a barn. Happily, in 1869 it was sold to John Darby Allcroft, a Worcester glove manufacturer and MP, who set about restoring it. The manorhouse is now in the care of English Heritage and is open daily (except for Mondays and Tuesdays in winter).

The Great Hall is a rare survival, almost untouched since medieval times and containing its original staircase, an open octagonal hearth and an innovative timber roof. Across the courtyard the delightful timber-framed gatehouse is decorated with carved animal heads.

The adjacent church, dedicated to St John the Baptist, was largely rebuilt between 1654 and 1664, following damage in the Civil War. This makes it more important than is immediately apparent, because very few churches were built or restored during this period. The south doorway is the only feature to have survived from the original Norman church.

STOKESAY CASTLE TO LUDLOW
Distance: 14.2km (9 miles)

Between Stokesay Castle and Ludlow the Way passes through Onibury and Stanton Lacy, two small and attractive villages. The former possesses a café (at the railway), a village shop and overnight accommodation, if needed.

Through the metal gate by which Stokesay Castle grounds are reached, turn right on a rough-surfaced lane to pass a farm. Continue on a track between hedgerows to a railway crossing on the Manchester to Cardiff line. Cross the line with care, and on the other side go left with the track for a short distance, until you can leave it, on the left, over a stile.

Beyond, go forward on a broad grassy track parallel with the railway line. In the next field climb a little to the right to go above a lightly-wooded slope, and after passing a couple of old limekilns start moving away from the railway line, heading for stiles ahead that take you across large pastures.

To the left the River Onny meanders across pastureland, set against the backdrop of wooded Whettleton Hill, on the summit of which there is an Iron Age hill-fort, Norton Camp.

The camp guarded the southern tip of Wenlock Edge and was defended by substantial ramparts and ditches, which now form the boundaries of adjoining fields to the east and south. The fort itself has become well-wooded, as are the steep slopes to its north and west – so steep that its occupants can have had little need to fear attack from these directions. The camp overlooked important trade routes and it has been suggested that tolls were extracted from travellers, though there is no evidence of this.

After crossing the second stile beyond the limekilns, bear right towards woodland, accessed by a waymarked stile.

In the woodland, bear left, ascending on a path that soon accompanies a post and wire fence to the top edge of the wood. At the top, bear left on a broad track that leads you on past Stokewood Farm. Just after the farm you meet its access, at a bend, and here cross the access and go over a stile. Head down the ensuing field, following the right field margin, to a stile in a hedgerow about 150m/yds away. Over this follow an enclosed and slightly overgrown path past Stokewood Cottage. Then go forward along a left field margin beside a fence/hedgerow, and continue doing so until you reach a lane.

Turn left down the lane towards the village of Onibury. When you reach a crossroads at the lodge to Stokesay Court, turn left to go down to the A49, and then left again to cross the River Onny and then the railway line once more.

Stokesay Court is a large neo-Elizabethan mansion of 1889 in a well-wooded park with some spectacular rhododendrons. The grounds are occasionally open to the public.

Leave the A49, and keep right, into the village, following the road round in front of the village shop and post office to pass the church of St Michael.

Onibury

Situated close to the River Onny, Onibury is a small village with a few attractive cottages in stone and half-timbering.

St Michael's Church is a lovely building (especially inside) which dates from the Norman period, but also contains work of the thirteenth, fourteenth and fifteenth centuries, though it was restored in 1902. Both Onibury and the River Onny take their name from a Welsh word 'on(n)', which means ash trees, but today there are more oaks than ash. Holly trees are unusually common in the area, a fact reflected in the name of a pub – The Hollybush – which once stood at Onibury. The Ilex Studio continues the tradition – 'ilex' is the Latin for 'holly'.

The Cardiff-Manchester railway passes Onibury but, sadly, trains no longer stop here. However, the handsome old station building has found a new lease of life as the Whistlestop Café, where accommodation is also available.

About 150m/yds after the church, turn left up a track leading to open fields at the top. Strike across the field, slightly left and between oak trees, to a metal kissing gate on the far side. Go forward across the top field edge beside a fence/hedgerow, to meet a lane. Turn left along the lane towards the hamlet of Walton, and after about 300m/yds, before reaching Walton, leave the lane, on the right, at a signposted stile just after a byway.

In the ensuing field go across to the right-hand hedgerow and follow this down two fields to cross a bridge. Over the bridge bear slightly left up to a stile at the end of a tall hedgerow, and then go alongside the hedgerow until it bears left. Keep on in the same direction across the field to a stile in a hedge. Go forward past a large old oak tree, and across a field, in the same direction, to a stile in a hedge corner. After the stile, turn left and go past another oak tree, and then across an arable field to a copse about 200m/yds distant, aiming for the left edge of it. Follow its boundary until you are level with a pond in its middle, and then strike left across the field to a stile beside a metal gate.

Beyond the stile, cross a lane to another stile opposite, and in the next field bear half-right towards a stile at a point midway between Pools Farm and Appletree Cottage. Cross a lane by stiles, and then go forward beside a hedge. When this doglegs go through a couple of metal gates, continuing in the same direction. Keep on until you meet the B4365. Before reaching the B-road, the path runs onto a track enclosed by hedgerows. When you reach the road, cross it, and go over a stile opposite.

opposite/...Stokesay Castle

Ludlow and Brown Clee Hill
Ludlow: the Butter Cross and the top of Broad Street

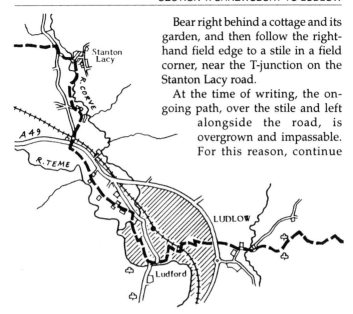

Bear right behind a cottage and its garden, and then follow the right-hand field edge to a stile in a field corner, near the T-junction on the Stanton Lacy road.

At the time of writing, the on-going path, over the stile and left alongside the road, is overgrown and impassable. For this reason, continue

following the hedgerow to a metal gate near a bridge over the River Corve on the edge of Stanton Lacy. Alternatively, turn right along the B4365 to the T-junction, and then go left into Stanton Lacy, but take care against approaching traffic on what is a high speed road.

Stanton Lacy

Stanton Lacy consists of a church, two farms and a picturesque huddle of houses and cottages set against a delightful green backdrop. The first church here was erected c680, according to legend, by St Milburgha, the Abbess of Wenlock Priory. The story is that she was being chased by a Welsh Prince determined to be her lover, and, having crossed the River Corve, she prayed that the water might become an impassable torrent. Her prayer was answered, the Prince was left stranded and in gratitude she founded the church on the site.

Whatever its origins, St Peter's is an impressive cruciform building which contains some unmistakable Saxon workmanship. The earliest parts of the church are the north and west walls of the nave and the north transept, which are decorated externally with lesenes or pilaster strips in a 'long and short' pattern, typical of mid-eleventh-century Saxon work, as are the tall, narrow proportions of the nave and transept. The moulding above the north door is also Saxon but reveals a Norman influence and probably does not pre-date the Conquest by many years. The dominant feature of the present church is the tower, which is believed to date from c1330 and was probably paid for by the Mortimers.

St Peter's is an unusually large church for such a small village but the explanation lies in the early prosperity of Stanton, which was the site of a Roman villa and continued to be intensively cultivated throughout the Saxon period. By the time of the Domesday survey it was at the centre of the richest, most productive land in Shropshire. At this time Stanton was held by the de Lacy family, close associates of William I. The manor later passed by marriage into the powerful hands of Roger Mortimer, first Earl of March, who was executed for treason in 1330. Today the patronage belongs to the Earl of Plymouth.

Go past the church and turn right on a broad track (signposted to Netherhope). When this bends right, leave it and cross a stile into a pasture to go forward beside a fence around the right-hand field margin. Your objective is a stile in the far right corner of the field, adjoining the River Corve. Across the stile keep on with the field margin until you can cross the river by a footbridge.

Over the footbridge turn left and stay along the field edge. When the accompanying river loops to the left, keep forward to rejoin it, and as you draw level with two isolated bushes in the field, bear half-right, aiming for the twin poles of a power line. Go just to the right of these and beneath the power lines to cross a ditch. Beyond the ditch, bear half-left to sparse woodland, entering it at a waymarked gate and stile, which give on to the edge of Ludlow Race Course and Golf Course.

The golf course was previously known as Old Field. Five Bronze Age tumuli (burial chambers or barrows) can be found on it, but these represent only a few of the barrows which are known to exist in the area between Stanton Lacy and Bromfield. There are at least twenty, as well as a cemetery of 130 shallow pits which was discovered during quarrying operations in 1966. Carbon dating indicated that human remains were buried here during the Bronze Age. The tumuli on Old Field were excavated by the Victorians, who found a bronze knife and evidence of cremation.

Turn left and follow a broad track around the edge of the race course. In the distance the tower of St Laurence's Church in Ludlow pinpoints the end of this section. To the south-west, the hills are cloaked in the trees of the Mortimer Forest.

Mortimer Forest is the name given by the Forestry Commission to its scattered holdings in northern Herefordshire and southern Shropshire. Though applied collectively, the name is also commonly used for the individual block of forest on the edge of Ludlow. The historical connection with the Mortimers is real enough, for the land encompassed by this term includes former Saxon hunting forests which were given by William I to Ralph Mortimer after the Conquest. Mortimer built a castle at Wigmore, and Ludlow later came into the family's hands too. For 300 years Ralph and his descendants ruled this part of the border country, and in the 1320s came close to ruling England too, because Roger Mortimer, the first Earl of March, was the lover of Edward II's wife, Queen Isabella, and played a leading role in the deposition and murder of the king in 1327. Isabella and Roger ruled in all but name during the minority of Edward's successor, Edward III, but in 1330 the eighteen-year-old king took control and had Mortimer executed for treason.

Though the emphasis in Mortimer Forest is very much on coniferous woodland, the Commission does manage the paths and rides with wildlife in mind. Broad verges open to the light encourage the growth of flowers, which attract butterflies, and the forest is known for its populations of commas and silver-washed fritillaries. It is also home to a unique, long-haired race of fallow deer. Despite much research, nobody is quite sure why they occur here and nowhere else, although it is believed the unique strain evolved after a single gene mutation. Sadly, it is now feared they could face extinction as a result of poaching. The BSE crisis has led to increased demand for venison and evidence that poachers are killing large numbers of deer, probably for the black market, was first discovered in August 1996.

The track eventually meets the B4365. Here, turn left and cross a railway bridge to meet the A49 at a T-junction. With care, cross the A49 to a hedge gap opposite. Ignore the signposted bridleway on the right, and keep forward along a field margin which 200m/yds further on bends to the left. The field edge path eventually leads to a gate. Beyond this keep on across a wide grassy strip of land as you pass Burway Farm. Go forward along the farm access track, soon to reach a surfaced lane. Cross the lane, and press on along a continuing track (waymarked and signposted), with Ludlow Castle and St Laurence's Church now forming a decorative frieze along the skyline ahead.

The track becomes surfaced and continues to meet the B4361 on the outskirts of Ludlow. When you reach the B-road, turn right, heading for the town centre, and after 50m/yds, at a bus stop sign on the right, turn right up steps and through a kissing gate to enter a pasture. Go half-left on a grassy path to another gate. Beyond this lies a bridge over a dry ditch, after which the path continues to another bridge (Burway Bridge), spanning the River Corve not far from its confluence with the River Teme.

Over the bridge go along a narrow path flanked by walls, to a gate, and there reach a rough track at the rear of houses. Turn left along this to a surfaced road that leads ahead into Ludlow. When the road bends right, leave it for a rising walkway and steps on the left. Turn left at the top of the steps, up a narrow street, and at its highest point turn right to pass beside the church and Hosyer's Almshouses to reach the town centre at the rear of the Butter Cross. A brief left and right brings you into the main street.

Go down Broad Street to pass under the archway at Broadgate, the only survivor of Ludlow's seven medieval gates. Beyond the gateway continue down Lower Broad Street to reach Ludford Bridge.

Ludlow

There is nowhere quite like Ludlow, Shropshire's (maybe Britain's) loveliest town. It's beautifully situated and its medieval street pattern, crammed with a total of 469 Listed Buildings, survives almost intact. It's possible there was a Saxon settlement on the site, but Ludlow's history really began about twenty years after the Norman Conquest when Roger de Lacy built a castle on a fine defensive site high above the confluence of Teme and Corve. A planned town was laid out in a grid pattern outside the castle gates and was soon a thriving centre.

The castle was later greatly extended and town walls were begun in 1233, enclosing the castle within their circuit, and making Ludlow one of just over a hundred towns in England and Wales to be fortified with a full circuit of walls.

Life must have been uncertain, given the continual power struggles of the Mortimers and their fellow Marcher lords, but Ludlow grew rich

Ludlow Castle

The River Teme at Ludlow

trading in wool and cloth and gained additional political importance during the Wars of the Roses, involvement in which was inevitable, given that the Earldom of March had passed to the Duke of York's son, Edward. The Lancastrian Henry VI took Ludlow in 1459 but in 1461 Edward, based at the Mortimers' former stronghold of Wigmore, marched to victory at Mortimer's Cross and then took the throne as Edward IV. Ludlow Castle now became Crown property and in 1472 it became the seat of the Council in the Marches of Wales, which was charged with the administration of this turbulent area. The king's two sons were sent to live at Ludlow but on his death in 1483 they were taken to London and murdered, achieving posthumous fame as the 'Princes in the Tower'.

Other Royal children were also brought up at Ludlow. Henry VII sent his sons Arthur and Henry to the castle, but Arthur died there in 1502, of natural causes, soon after his marriage by proxy to Catherine of Aragon. The Prince's body was taken to Worcester Cathedral for burial but his heart was interred in Ludlow Church. Catherine was betrothed and later married to his brother, the future Henry VIII, an event which would later provide Henry with the opportunity to break with Rome and establish the Church of England. Henry's daughter Mary (later 'Bloody Mary') lived at Ludlow for a time too.

Ludlow was the last Shropshire castle to hold out for Charles I in the Civil War, not surrendering until June 1646 when the Parliamentarian cannons on Whitcliffe Common battered it into submission. The King's nephew, Prince Rupert, was its commander for a time, and much later, during the reign of Charles II, he returned to become Lord President of the Council in the Marches, but the Council was abolished in 1689 and Ludlow Castle left to decay. It was acquired by the Earl of Powis in 1811, and essential repairs were made. Today it's open to the public and well worth a visit, both for its own intrinsic interest and atmosphere, and for the fine views from its topmost tower.

Even after the Council was abolished the town continued to prosper and became a fashionable social centre for wealthy county families in the eighteenth and nineteenth centuries. Glove making was now the major industry, reaching a peak in 1814, when 660,000 gloves were produced.

Today, Ludlow still thrives as energetically as ever, mainly through light industry, livestock sales and tourism, and is renowned for the superb festival it stages for a fortnight every summer, the highlight of which is the twice-daily performance of a Shakespeare play in the ruined castle, recalling the fact that it was at Ludlow Castle in 1634 that John

Milton's celebrated masque 'Comus' was given its first performance.

As you approach Ludlow on the Shropshire Way church and castle dominate the skyline together and it's easy to see that St Laurence's is the largest and most majestic parish church in Shropshire. Yet, despite this, the church is scarcely visible from the town centre, so hemmed in is it by buildings. It's well worth seeking out as you explore the town for it has the stature almost of a small cathedral. It dates from the twelfth century but most of what exists today is fifteenth-century and was built with profits from the wool trade. There are many fine monuments and furnishings inside, and a memorial stone to A E Housman is to be found on the exterior wall near the north door, but it is most notable for its fourteenth- and fifteenth-century misericords.

Nearly all Ludlow's buildings are beautiful, but some particularly notable ones which should be sought out include the Reader's House, Hosyer's Almshouses, the Butter Cross, the Tolsey and Dinham House. The most-photographed building in town is the magnificent Feathers Hotel, once the home of Rees Jones from Pembrokeshire who served as an attorney at the Council in the Marches. It became an inn in 1670 and is captivating, inside and out. The oldest pub in town, however, is the Bull Hotel.

Broad Street, lined with elegant Georgian houses, is described by Pevsner as 'one of the most memorable streets in England' and it's a great pity that it's allowed to be dominated these days by parked cars. The Broad Gate itself, one of seven which once guarded the town walls, still stands, with the addition of an attractive castellated house built over it in the eighteenth century.

Ludford is a tiny hamlet missed by most visitors to Ludlow but it's a picturesque place, well worth a closer look. Just the other side of fifteenth-century Ludford Bridge, the small cluster of buildings includes a Norman church and an almshouse, St Giles's Hospital, founded in 1216. The Old Bell is a timber-framed house of 1614, which was once a pub, and Ludford House is an impressive building which is either late Elizabethan or early Jacobean. From Ludford you can walk up onto Whitcliffe Common and enjoy superb views of Ludlow before returning to town via Dinham Bridge, which spans the Teme below the castle.

SECTION 2: LUDLOW TO IRONBRIDGE

Between Ludlow, the southernmost point of the Shropshire Way, and Ironbridge, the route occupies itself with yet more high ground, this time passing over Titterstone Clee and Brown Clee. The benefit of height enables you to see much of the surrounding countryside, a pattern of patchwork fields from which the towns and villages protrude gracefully. Distant views towards the Black Country are less inspiring, but are sufficiently far away to be ignored.

Beyond the Clees the route meanders on across Wenlock Edge, which inspired Vaughan Williams to write *On Wenlock Edge*, a song cycle of the poems from Housman's *A Shropshire Lad*.

> *On Wenlock Edge the wood's in trouble;*
> *His forest fleece the Wrekin heaves;*
> *The gale, it plies the saplings double,*
> *And thick on Severn snow the leaves.*

A visit to the charming town of Much Wenlock preludes the final stage of this section up to the historically important town of Ironbridge.

Logistically, this section of the walk is the most problematic. Small villages – Knowbury, Holdgate and Easthope – are passed through, but offer little sustenance to walkers. Not until Much Wenlock is reached can supplies be replenished, without a diversion. The closure of the Wheathill Youth Hostel in 1998 means that between Ludlow and Wilderhope Manor there is very limited accommodation.

Between Ludlow and Wilderhope Manor, the Way also tackles two high summits, the Clee Hills, and although the distance from Ludlow to Wilderhope (31.5km/19½ miles) is not excessive, the additional effort of getting over the two hills should be allowed for, especially in less than ideal walking weather. It may be worth considering using a bus or a taxi and breaking the section by returning to Ludlow for an additional overnight stay.

Until the accommodation infrastructure along the Shropshire Way is more fully developed, the problems of finding somewhere to stay overnight will remain.

LUDLOW TO KNOWBURY
Distance: 7.2km (4½ miles)

The Way continues from Ludford Bridge by heading along Temeside. Walk beside the river, turning right at the first road junction and following the road round into Weeping Cross Lane. Go up to the T-junction at the top.

[For walkers staying overnight in the centre of town, this same point may be reached more speedily from the Butter Cross by going left into King Street and ahead through the Bull Ring into Tower Street, then branching right into Lower Galdeford at the bottom of which, near a large car park, you meet Weeping Cross Lane at its junction with Sheet Road. Go forward.]

Turn right along Sheet Road as far as a telephone kiosk and go through a tunnel beneath the railway. As you exit the tunnel, ignore a footpath sign and keep forward on a surfaced path that bends to the right to meet an estate road. Turn right, and follow this round until the next turning on the right, going past house number 58, and then immediately left to reach an open area. Go straight ahead uphill to a surfaced lane (Dark Lane).

Go left along the lane at the rear of houses, and shortly turn right at a footpath sign to enter another housing estate. Keep forward, crossing two estate roads and go on to reach Parys Road on the edge of Sheet Road Industrial Estate. Turn right for 100m/yds, with a glimpse of Titterstone Clee Hill appearing beyond the industrial estate, and then go left down Coder Road.

When Coder Road bends left, keep ahead between fences to reach the Ludlow by-pass. Here you are deflected left to a stile. Cross the by-pass with great care, and go down steps on the other side to another stile. Keep forward along the right-hand edge of a large pasture to a double stile, and continue in the same direction to a lane (double stile). Go down the lane to Ledwyche Bridge.

Beyond the bridge press on along the lane to a large building on the left, and here, as the road bends left, leave it for a broad track on the right. A short distance further on, keep forward, with Ledwyche Pool on your left. The on-going track goes on into the edge of Ledwyche Covert, and as you leave it a fine view of Titterstone Clee appears directly ahead.

Over to your right at this point is a tree-clad hill crowned by an Iron Age fort, Caynham Camp. The site was defended by formidable ramparts and ditches and its occupants also had the benefit of far-reaching views, with the forts on the Clee Hills just some of the other encampments visible. The village of Caynham lies on the far side of the hill and is believed to have been one of the first places in Shropshire to be settled by the Anglo-Saxons.

Keep ahead along an obvious track at the bottom of a field. When you reach a low hedgerow on the right, turn right, keeping to the left of the hedgerow. When this ends, go forward through a gap in a larger hedgerow, across a brook, and turn right beside the brook to reach a stile next to a gate. Go into the ensuing field and cross Cay Brook by a footbridge. Bear left, climbing slightly, and then keep forward to a stile by a gate on the far side of a field.

Now go to the left of two isolated trees in the middle of a large pasture. As you draw level with the nearest of these, keep forward, targeting Knowbury church on the raised skyline ahead. The pasture is pathless, but eventually you intersect a farm access near a gate. Turn right along the track to pass through a gap in a hedgerow about 100m/yds away. Through the gap, ignore the prominent track going left, and go forward along a hedgerow. As you approach the highest point of this short ascent, turn left on a signposted, broad, green track across arable land, once again heading for Knowbury church.

Go through a hedge gap and turn right, along a field margin and immediately left keeping on beside a field drainage channel to a stile. Go forward in the ensuing field, initially heading for a group of buildings, but gradually bearing towards the top right corner of the field where there is a stile. Beyond this keep on up to the top of the next field where another stile gives access to a lane.

Turn right and follow the lane to a signposted footpath on the left, flanked on the right by an outstanding holly hedge. Cross a stile at the top, and go forward, with a hedgerow on your right, to a gap. Keep forward along a hedge to a gate, and forward again to a lane adjoining Knowbury church.

Given its pastoral setting, you would expect Knowbury to be an agricultural village but it actually developed as an industrial community. In the late seventeenth century iron ore was mined at Knowbury and transported to Bringewood (now part of Mortimer Forest) where it was smelted

Titterstone Clee Hill from Caynham

in charcoal furnaces. Later, local furnaces were established and quite an important ironworks developed in the nineteenth century. Coal mining and limestone quarrying provided other employment for the population and there were also clay pits, a tile works and a brickyard in the nineteenth and early twentieth centuries.

With so much industry, squatting flourished and some of the cottages and smallholdings are still owned by descendants of the squatters, many of whom came from the Black Country and South Wales. The main principle of squatting was that if a man could erect a house between sunrise and sunset the land was his. In practice, the main thing was to get a fire going so that smoke could be seen issuing from a chimney. For this reason you can usually identify a squatter's cottage by the size of its chimney stack, which was built first and therefore had to be large enough to be a freestanding structure. The rest of the house could then be built onto it in a slightly more leisurely fashion.

Knowbury used to be split between the parishes of Caynham and Bitterley and it wasn't until 1839 that it acquired its own church, when

St Paul's was built. The parish of Knowbury came into existence the following year when the church was consecrated.

Knowbury House is the home of Major Adrian Coles who founded the British Hedgehog Preservation Society in 1982. The society's car stickers will be familiar to many people but one of its greatest successes has been in persuading numerous landowners to install escape ramps in the pits below cattle grids, into which many hapless hedgehogs tumble. Without a ramp they are unable to climb out and will die of starvation.

KNOWBURY TO HOLDGATE
Distance: 19.8km (12¼ miles)

Cross the road and go up the surfaced turning area beside the church, to a step stile, and along a pathway between fences. At the top of the path, bear left in a large open pasture, with Titterstone Clee Hill in the distance. A narrow path curves round the top of a slope, though the right of way descends to a stile at the lane into Knowbury, and then climbs back up again, heading for Titterstone Clee Hill.

The path rises slightly as it approaches a hedgerow and then crosses a waymarked stile. Cross three narrow fields and the top of an old sunken lane, and go over the next field to another stile. In the next field keep forward with a delightful holly hedgerow on your right. Go through a hedge gap and continue with the holly hedge to another stile, hidden in a corner. Go down into a small wooded dingle and cross a stile and a brook, rising on the other side to walk below a post and rail fence. Keep left beside the fence to meet vehicle track. Turn right on this, and at a cross-track a short way on, keep forward to reach a corner of a large open pasture. Go up-field with a fence on your left. When the fence bends left, keep on in much the same direction, aiming just to the left of farm buildings ahead, where there is a stile at a barn corner. Cross this and bear left on a gravel access track leading out to a road.

Beside the track you may notice heaps of coal and iron slag, evidence of the industries which used to be the main source of employment here.

[Walkers in need of refreshment should note that as you reach the road there is a pub 400m/yds away if you turn left, and Cleehill village, with shops, pubs, tea shop and a chippy, about 1km (three-quarters of a mile) to the right.]

Cross the road (A4117) and walk along the lane opposite (Dhustone Lane) for about 400m/yds to a bend. At the bend, leave the lane, over a cattle grid and onto a vehicle track. At the top of the track, as it veers towards a modern house, keep forward on a broad grassy track beside a hedgerow to a metal gate.

Beyond the gate, bear half-left in the ensuing pasture to the top left corner, aiming for Shop Farm. Go through another metal gate, and pass the farmhouse to reach a series of sheep pens beyond which you enter a large open pasture. Cross this in the same direction to a fence/stile. Keep on in the next field to a dark-blue metal gate in a corner beside a holly tree. Beyond the gate, turn

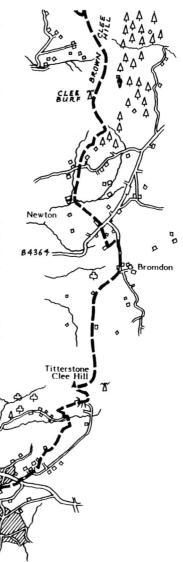

*Looking across to Brown Clee Hill
from the top of Titterstone Clee Hill*

right and cross a small culvert to access a large open pasture dotted with gorse bushes.

Keep parallel with the right-hand fence, deviating only as necessary to avoid dense gorse bushes, and keep on to the top right corner of the field. Over a stile, in the next field, pick a way through more gorse, descending half-left on an indistinct path, aiming (if you can see it) just to the right of the trig pillar on Titterstone Clee Hill ahead; nearby overhead power lines also serve as a useful guide to a waymarked stile over a fence. In the next field keep forward along the right-hand field margin, and at the top of the field disregard the stile and gate on the right near Nine Springs Farm, and turn left, going down-field beside a hedgerow on your right to a waymarked gate.

Through the gate descend right to a footbridge spanning Benson's Brook, and then rise on the opposite side through bracken. Cross a rough-surfaced lane, and keep forward on a broad green track, with a fence on the left, and follow the track as it cuts across open bracken-covered moorland to a tunnel through the Bitterley Incline. When you reach the tunnel, climb to the left of it to gain the Incline, and turn right along it, ascending to the track head at a large level area with numerous derelict and dismantled buildings.

Titterstone Quarries were begun in the 1880s for the purpose of extracting dhustone, the local name for a type of hard basalt used for road building. The quarries were served by the Bitterley Incline, which the Shropshire Way briefly joins. At Bitterley Wharf it connected with the Dhustone Incline (which the Shropshire Way crosses just after Shop Farm) and the main line to Ludlow, enabling dhustone to be transported all over the country. Only in the 1950s did new road building techniques put an end to dhustone's dominance. The quarry industry continues on the southern slopes of Clee Hill but at a reduced level with the works well hidden within a dip in the hill.

Bear right through this unsightly hiatus to meet a stony track at a bend. Rise left on this to pass through the dismantled abutments of a quarry tramway and continue to reach the summit radar station's access road at a hairpin bend. Cross the access road twice,

Abdon Burf, the main summit of Brown Clee Hill, from Nordy Bank

keeping forward to an ascending stony track that leads you to the brink of a large disused quarry. Turn left up the edge of this on a grassy path that leads you towards two flat-topped radar dishes that are operated by the National Air Traffic Services, and about 100m/yds beyond the second of these you reach the trig pillar on the summit (533m/1,749ft).

Locals say that the view from Titterstone Clee Hill (often simply known as Clee Hill) is the best in England, and, on a clear day, it's hard to disagree, as you look from Cannock Chase to the Brecon Beacons, from Snowdonia to the Cotswolds. In the right weather conditions it's stunning. Among the many individual hills you can pick out are the distinctive shapes of pine-crested May Hill (Gloucestershire), whale-backed Bredon Hill (Worcestershire) and the strange broken cone of Ysgyryd Fawr (Monmouthshire). You can look back at those Shropshire hills you've already tackled and forward to those, such as Wenlock Edge, the Wrekin, and, of course, Brown Clee, which are still to come.

The Clee Hills are composed of Old Red Sandstone topped by coal measures and a capping of dhustone. Coal, iron, and stone have been worked here since the thirteenth century but until the 1850s the primary industry was coal. In medieval times it was mined from simple bell pits, as it was close to the surface. By the eighteenth century much of the surface coal had gone and more sophisticated techniques were used. As the coalfields expanded so did related industries such as brick, glass and pottery making, lime burning and iron forging. Quarrying also increased dramatically. By the time of the railway age Clee Hill was so industrialised that it was provided with a branch line from Ludlow.

While it's all too obvious that Titterstone is horribly scarred with the detritus of industry, not to mention the radar installation, it remains a strangely compelling place with a powerful presence. The summit is marked by a craggy outcrop of dhustone, falling steeply to a scree-strewn slope, and the Giant's Chair, a rocky outcrop looking north to Brown Clee, and so named because it is composed of boulders supposedly dropped by a passing giant.

The largest hill-fort ever built in the Marches once occupied the entire flat top of Clee Hill, and the tumbled stone foundations of the encircling rampart can still be seen in places. It was big enough to have housed as many as 3,000 people in densely packed rows of huts.

Much of Titterstone is unenclosed common land on which the commoners' stock is free to roam. There is a fair network of paths and it's great walking country. It also benefits from a variety of wildlife habitats, some of them created by man, such as the cliff faces in the quarries. The different types of rock add further variety. One of the rarest habitats is the block scree beneath the Giant's Chair, formed at the end of the last Ice Age and now encrusted with lichens, mosses and ferns.

The coal measures produce an acid soil which supports such distinctive plants as cotton grass and sundew. In drier areas gorse is dominant and flowers for much of the year. A fair variety of birds can be seen, including the increasingly rare skylark, and there's no better place to watch buzzards soaring high above or to listen for the harsh cry of the raven.

From the trig pillar head off on an obvious green path in a roughly north-easterly direction until you are past the two flat-topped radar dishes. Start heading in a more northerly direction, and descend the north-facing slopes of Titterstone Clee Hill obliquely to an obvious green track through bracken, heading directly for Brown Clee in the far distance.

Take care descending the northern slope, which is mainly grassy but punctuated with dhustone boulders that can be slippery when wet. Having reached the green track keep following it, descending roughly northwards and heading for the red-roofed buildings of Callowgate Farm.

Just past the farm you reach a gate at the head of a sunken lane (often muddy). Go forward down this (Callow Lane), and keep on until it meets a minor lane at Bromdon. Turn left and go along the lane, past Upper Bromdon Farm, and start climbing easily to the high point along the lane.

From the high point, keep on for 150m/yds and then leave the lane, turning left on the access to The Knapp Farm. As you approach the farm, leave the access, turning right at a signpost, and going down a field edge to a gate and stile. Beyond this go slightly right up the ensuing field to another step stile, near Dodshill Farm. Over the stile, turn immediately left, and follow a rough access track out to meet the B4364 at Dodshill.

Having reached the road, turn right along it for 20m/yds, then go left at a footpath signpost, heading down a rough-surfaced track.

The hedge-lined track descends gently towards Newton Dingle, and then climbs again to a fork near Newton Farm. Here, branch right, still on a broad track, that now rises steadily between hedgerows to pass Newton Cottage, where the rough surfacing gives way to a grassy track that runs on to meet a lane near a telephone box. Cross the lane, slightly right, and go up a signposted footpath between overgrown hedgerows.

The path continues to rise to an isolated farm, and then goes right on a green holloway. After 150m/yds this meets two gates above The Toot. Go through the left-hand gate (wooden) to continue on a path between banks of gorse, still on a sunken way.

The way rises to a metal gate, and beyond it crosses the top of Old Lodge Coppice, a mixed woodland, mainly beech with a few pine, spruce and larch. The path keeps to the outer edge of the woodland, passing between heather, gorse and bilberries. As it cuts across upland pasture, head for the twin towers of a navigational relay station on Clee Burf.

The on-going path rises directly to the edge of a part-fenced quarry, and then bears right towards a gate to the right of the relay station. Beyond the gate go forward along the top edge of Castle Covert, following the line of a wall/fence on a grassy path that passes through an area of low dolerite boulders, where there has been extensive bell pit mining. One or two of the pits are close to the path, and care is needed to avoid them in poor visibility.

Keep following the wallside path, which is a little boggy in places. Gradually both wall/fence and path descend. As you approach a fence junction near Five Springs the line of the Shropshire Way starts to move away slightly from the wall/fence to a 'jump' stile a short distance to the right of a metal gate. Most walkers, however, tend to use the gate and the on-going path beyond (ahead, not left) that leads to a fence corner at Sandy Nap.

(If you do use the 'jump' stile, then once over it aim slightly left across open upland pasture and bracken to intercept the pronounced track rising from the gate.) From Sandy Nap the path runs on beside the fence to meet another path branching left and right, where the Shropshire Way turns left.

[Walkers wanting to visit the summit of Brown Clee Hill, Abdon Burf, should branch right at this point and walk up to and back from the summit. Additional distance: 1km/half a mile.]

Brown Clee Hill is the highest summit in Shropshire, and one of ten 'Marilyns' in Shropshire, for those walkers who like to collect such summits: the others are Stiperstones, Titterstone Clee Hill, Long Mynd (Pole Bank), Caer Caradoc, Heath Mynd, the Wrekin, Burrow, Callow Hill and View Edge (otherwise known as Weo Edge).

The Clee Hills were once part of a Royal forest, Clee Forest, which lost its Royal

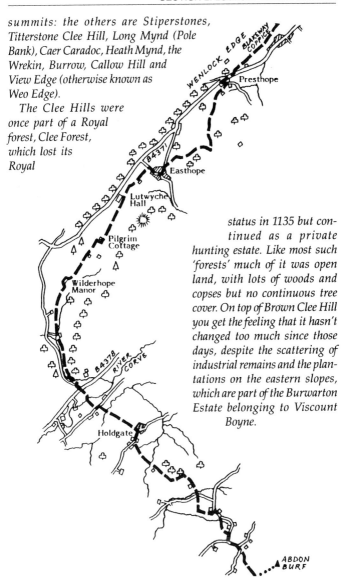

status in 1135 but continued as a private hunting estate. Like most such 'forests' much of it was open land, with lots of woods and copses but no continuous tree cover. On top of Brown Clee Hill you get the feeling that it hasn't changed too much since those days, despite the scattering of industrial remains and the plantations on the eastern slopes, which are part of the Burwarton Estate belonging to Viscount Boyne.

Brown Clee is bigger and more beautiful than Titterstone, though its outline is less distinctive and somehow it gives the impression of being lower. It has two tops, Clee Burf and Abdon Burf, and like Titterstone, has been exploited for its mineral wealth for centuries. Both the eastern slopes and the top are pocked with shallow depressions and mounds which mark the site of bell pits, an early form of mining which consisted of digging a short shaft and working the seam from the foot of it as far as was safe, leaving a pit with a bell-shaped profile. It is believed to have been the highest coalfield in England.

Quarrying has left its mark on Brown Clee too, though not so severely as on its twin, and it ceased altogether in 1936. Ironstone was dug from the coal measures from the medieval period and fed a number of forges encircling the hill. More recently, it was the dhustone which was exploited and the ruins of a stone crushing plant disfigure Abdon Burf. Wagons on a steep incline transported the stone down towards the railway at Ditton Priors, a village lying to the north-east.

People have lived on Brown Clee since the earliest times. There was a large Iron Age fort on Abdon Burf and a smaller settlement on Clee Burf, both of which have been destroyed by quarrying. Look down to the lower slopes on the western side, however, and you will see the unmistakable outline of another fort, Nordy Bank. Its ramparts are well-preserved but not particularly formidable and it was possibly a look-out post for the larger forts on top.

From the summit of Brown Clee in 1940 were scattered the ashes of Simon Evans; postman, poet and short story writer of Cleobury Mortimer. After being wounded and gassed in the First World War he sought peace and healing in the Shropshire countryside where his daily round on foot in the Rea Valley allowed him to breathe in pure air and to compose poetry at the same time.

The view from Shropshire's highest hill is all you would expect and includes the Malverns, Cotswolds, Black Mountains, Brecon Beacons, Clent Hills, Cannock Chase, the Black Country, Wyre Forest, the Wrekin, the Breidden Hills, Wenlock Edge, Long Mynd, Radnor Forest, the Berwyns, and even Cader Idris on clear days.

From the summit, return to the collapsed wall, and go forward through an old fenceline, immediately branching left to cross a stile (though there is evidence that many walkers simply continue ahead, without crossing the stile, to reach a track below).

Over the stile, bear right around the edge of an area of gorse bushes until you meet a metal gate. Through this you join an old track known locally as an outrack or straker way.

At one time all of the hillside above the encircling roads was common land divided between several parishes, while an outer ring of parishes also had grazing rights. Stock from these outer parishes was driven to and from Brown Clee on tracks known as outracks or straker ways, most of which now do good service as footpaths and bridleways. Some of them are deeply sunken with long use.

Follow the track down to meet a lane. As you descend, the Wrekin once more comes into view to the north-east, while to the north-west lie Wenlock Edge, the Stretton Hills and the Long Mynd.

At the lane, turn right, and go down to pass a telephone box, turning left at a T-junction onto the lane to Abdon and Tugford. Follow the lane and take the next turning on the right (signposted to Earnstrey), and after about 300m/yds, leave the lane, on the left, over a stile. Go forward along the top edge of a field, beside a fence. This guides you on to walk beside a holloway with a brook in it, before curving right to head down to the bottom of the field. At the bottom, go left and cross a footbridge, and then ascend on the other side along the continuation of the holloway, to a stile beside a gate. Beyond this you reach another lane.

Turn left, and walk as far as the first farm on the left (New Earnstrey Park Farm). Just as you approach the farm, leave the lane, left, over a stile, and go forward along a field margin until, after the last of the farm outbuildings, you can turn right over another stile.

The name Earnstrey comes from the Old English for 'eagle's tree' but it may be that the 'eagles' were actually buzzards. New Earnstrey Park is a very old house which was encased in brick in Elizabethan times and is believed to be one of the two earliest brick houses in the county (the other is Plaish Hall, near Cardington). There was a Norman deer park at Earnstrey at one time, which occupied much the same area as an earlier Saxon hunting estate. The Norman park was enclosed by an embankment, traces of which are still visible in places.

Go down three fields, and part way down the third, turn right over a stile and footbridge. On the other side, walk beside the on-going hedge to reach another stile, beyond which go slightly right across the next field to a stile near a telephone pole. Cross a lane and go down a track opposite, rising gently to reach and pass

Earnstrey Hall Farm.

A short way on, go through the right-hand one of two metal gates, and forward down the ensuing field beside a fence on the left. Through another gate, keep on for a short distance further, until you can turn left through a gate near the top edge of a wooded slope.

Just at this point there is a fine view across the patterned green and red fields of Corve Dale, with the village of Holdgate neatly surrounded by trees.

Through the gate go forward across the top edge of the wooded slope until you meet a waymark at the far end of the woodland (Mittons Rough). Stride on a little further, then bear half-right, downhill on a grassy rake through bracken, and across an open slope dotted with a few trees to a stile in a hedgerow below.

Beyond the stile, go straight down the ensuing pasture to another stile to the left of a gate. Beyond this keep on in the same direction to a hedge corner. From the corner keep on with the hedgerow on your left, until you can cross it at a stile, and switch to the other side. Keep going in the same direction, passing at a distance the isolated house of Blue Hall. Eventually, you cross another stile and footbridge to go forward along an old green lane flanked by hedgerows.

The hedge guides you to another stile and fence. Beyond, go on, slightly right across the ensuing field to a hedge corner near a gate, and keep on to another gate. Go up to the right of farm buildings ahead to reach the edge of Holdgate village at a gate. Turn right along the lane to the church of the Holy Trinity.

Though a small, isolated village today, Holdgate was previously of greater importance. It's named after the Norman Helgot, who was given the manor after the Conquest. Recognising the strategic value of this ridge overlooking Corve Dale, he built a motte and bailey castle which was one of the few Shropshire castles mentioned in the Domesday survey of 1086. His son, Herbert FitzHelgot, entertained Henry I here in 1109. The castle was later sold to Robert Burnell, Chancellor of England. In 1280 he built a new stone castle in the bailey of the old wooden one. All that remains now is a high, tree-clad mound, and a tower which was incorporated into a farmhouse, built within the former bailey after the castle had fallen into decay in the seventeenth century. The fields on the other side of the lane are marked by slight earthworks which reveal where the houses of the much larger medieval village stood.

Holy Trinity Church has a twelfth-century nave and thirteenth-century chancel and tower, a richly decorated south doorway (possibly by the renowned Hereford School of carvers, active in the twelfth century) and various features from later periods. On the exterior south chancel wall is a sheela-na-gig, a pagan fertility figure, and inside are some interesting misericords, one depicting dragons, and also a font with a dragon carving. The sheela-na-gig is particularly interesting because it is such a rare feature in England (though common in Ireland). There are eighteen known sheela-na-gigs in England, and four of those are in Shropshire. The others are at Church Stretton, and at neighbouring Tugford, where there are two.

HOLDGATE TO EASTHOPE
Distance: 8km (5 miles)

Go through the metal gate beside the church, and down the ensuing field, initially on a concrete track and then on a grassy trod to a stile. Over the stile, bear left, and keep following the field edge, which contains a number of old oak trees, down to meet Trow Brook.

Cross the brook on stepping stones, occasionally flooded, and then go forward along the right-hand edge of a large pasture to a stile in a corner which brings you onto a lane. Cross the lane and go left through a metal gate, following the field boundary round to meet the River Corve, crossed by a wide bridge. Over the bridge, bear right, and follow the right-hand field edge up-field to a stile giving on to the B4368.

Turn right for 30m/yds, and then left on a minor road to Longville, as the route starts to head for Wenlock Edge. Go down this road for about 100m/yds, and then leave it, on the right, over a stile. Bear left in the ensuing field, and go down to a bridge over a brook, near New House Farm. Immediately over the bridge turn left, and then follow the course of the brook for some distance across fields below the wooded slopes of Stanway Coppice, until waymarks guide you towards a narrow footbridge near Lower Stanway Farm.

Much of Stanway Coppice belongs to the National Trust, though it represents just a small part of their extensive holdings on Wenlock Edge. It is probably due to the Trust that so much of the Edge retains its cloak of ancient woodland, of which Stanway is a valuable part. It is noted for the richness of its ground flora, with such species as great woodrush, dog's mercury, wood melick and the delicately beautiful wood sorrel, something of a Shropshire speciality.

Over the footbridge cross a stile, and go forward between the brook and a fence to meet the farm access. Turn right, re-cross the brook, and then go immediately left over another stile, and forward along a field, parallel with the brook. Keep going until more stiles and a footbridge take you back over the brook and into another field. Keep following the course of the brook, and you will be guided to a substantial footbridge, where the youth hostel at Wilderhope Manor comes into view.

Go forward over the footbridge and along a gently rising field edge, and follow this round to reach a farm access at the top of the field, near Wilderhope Farm. Continue towards the manor, but leaving the prominent farm track near barns to pass to the right of them, and so reach a stile at the entrance to the manor grounds.

Wilderhope Manor belongs to the National Trust but is leased to the YHA, and it's hard to imagine a lovelier place to stay the night. With its gables and projecting circular stairwell, this is the finest of the old houses along Wenlock Edge. It was built of local limestone about 1535 and its appearance has changed little since. Notable interior features include an original spiral staircase and some superb plaster ceilings. During the Civil War it was the home of a Major Smallman who escaped a posse of Roundheads near Presthope by making his horse jump from Wenlock Edge. The horse was killed but the Major escaped and the site of the incident is known as Major's Leap.

Beautiful as the house is, it's the setting which really makes it. The Wilderhope Estate comprises a landscape of wooded stream valleys, flower-rich grassland, ancient woodland, copses and old hedgerows. Ash, oak, spindle, spurge laurel and yew grow in the woods, the grasslands support such charming flowers as eyebright and salad burnet, and the hedges along the old trackways are thick with hazel, dogwood, rose, elder and blackthorn. A number of fields show the ridge and furrow pattern which indicates they were once subject to the plough in the Middle Ages.

Pass either right or left of the manor, and on the far side stay on the on-going broad track as it swings left and heads across fields to a T-junction near Pilgrim Cottage.

Not surprisingly, a story lies behind the unusual name of this house, whose occupants, together with those of a nearby row of cottages, long since gone, are said to have sailed on the Mayflower to the New World in 1624. The house itself is either much altered since that time, or a later one has been built on the same site.

Turn right and go past Pilgrim Cottage, and then immediately left on a broad track striking down a field edge.

On your right, as you approach Lutwyche Hall, the woodland of Mogg Forest clothes the Edge, concealing the ramparts of yet another Iron Age fort, The Ditches, built in the first or second century BC. Local tradition has it that the Druids were active here but there's no evidence of this. Below the trees is the intriguingly named Murder Pool, which may (or may not) have some connection with a murder carried out at nearby Easthope in 1333 when the vicar killed the church's patron, John de Easthope.

Lutwyche Hall is a gabled mansion originally dating from 1587, but extended and altered in the eighteenth century. Mellow brick towers flank the main entrance and there are fine mullioned windows. The house suffered a recent tragedy when, in 1989, after seven years of careful restoration work, a fire caused substantial damage. Like many houses of its vintage, Lutwyche Hall is said to be haunted, both by the ghost of Sir Edward Lutwyche, a seventeenth-century judge, and by that of an unidentified woman who moves furniture around. The novelist, short story and travel writer Stella Benson (1892-1933) was born here. After her death, her brother George Reginald Benson inherited the hall and also produced a novel, 'Brother Wolf'. The house enjoys a fine setting, looking out across Hope Dale to Mogg Forest.

The on-going track leads past Lutwyche Hall, and forward to Hall Farm. As you reach the barns of the farm, go to the right over a stile into a large open pasture. Turn left beside open barns and go forward along a fenceline on your left. When the fence bears away to the left, continue in the same direction on a broad green track that guides you to a stile beside a metal gate.

Beyond the gate, go forward along a vehicle track beside a wooden fence. The track eventually runs on to meet the lane into Easthope. Turn right and go down to the village, following the lane through the village to the church of St Peter.

A small and very secluded village, Easthope has a few buildings of great interest, including the Manor House (c1600) and, opposite it, a cruck-framed cottage. Manor Farm originated in the thirteenth century when it was built as a cell for monks from nearby Wenlock Priory. The Malthouse, built from oak timbers infilled with locally made brick, retains a fourteenth-century hall, altered in the fifteenth, which is the only Shropshire example of the medieval cross-wing type of building, and of great architectural importance.

St Peter's Church has immensely thick limestone walls and inside there is an hour-glass beside the pulpit, a reminder of an old and tactful tradition which sought to discourage the delivery of long sermons. The date on its bracket is 1662 but it is a replica of the original, which was destroyed in a fire in 1923. Though St Peter's has a twelfth-century nave and a chancel of c1300, most of it was rebuilt after the fire.

The circular shape of the churchyard probably indicates that it was a site of pre-Christian religious significance. It seems a peaceful place but is said to be haunted by three ghosts. One of these was Will Garmston, a vicar of the church who murdered its patron in 1333. The other two were monks who killed each other in a drunken fight. Their bodies are said to lie in the two uninscribed graves (except for a cross on each one) under a yew tree.

EASTHOPE TO MUCH WENLOCK
Distance: 8.8km (5½ miles)

Leave Easthope on the Much Wenlock road, and about 200m/yds out of the village, leave the road and branch right onto a vehicle track. At a double gate, keep forward and follow the right-hand field hedge round to a stile beside a gate. In the next pasture, go half-left below Natal Coppice to a signpost, and then on across to the far side of the pasture to a concealed stile in a field corner.

The stile is at the bottom edge of an ascending path, rising through a narrow strip of undergrowth. At the top stile, go left, descending along the margin of an arable field to Dove Plantation. Go down through the edge of the plantation, emerging at the bottom into another large field. Walk down beside a hedgerow on your left until, near a pond, you can turn right to follow a fenceline and later a hedgerow into a broad hedgeway near two old oak trees. By means of a stile you enter another narrow linking neck of woodland.

Beyond, strike across an arable field to a pond surrounded by trees in mid-field, and keep on from there in the same direction to a broad vehicle track on the other side. Follow this out, passing a large shed on the right, and shortly, when the track forks just before a gate, branch right and walk out to meet the Bourton road. Turn left and walk uphill to a T-junction with the B4371. Turn right for Much Wenlock, taking care, in the absence of a footpath, against approaching traffic.

Go past the turning for Hughley and Church Preen, and soon leave the road by turning into the Wenlock Edge car park.

Wenlock Edge is one of the most distinctive features of the Shropshire landscape, though best seen from the west where it appears as an unbroken escarpment running from Benthall Edge to Craven Arms. From the east it is more elusive as it rises almost imperceptibly as a gently swelling ridge. Within its basic ridge structure it seems to form a series of waves, and actually consists for much of its length of two parallel edges, with Hope Dale between them.

The Silurian limestone of which Wenlock Edge is composed was formed about 420 million years ago in a tropical sea. It probably originated south of the equator and has moved north due to continental drift. Developing as a barrier reef on the edge of a continental shelf, it was built up largely from the accumulation of sediments and the skeletons of marine creatures such as corals, brachiopods and crinoids. Earth movements and erosion have created the escarpment as it exists today.

Throughout England, limestone supports a rich flora, and Wenlock Edge is no exception. The thin soils that have developed are colonised by a very distinctive range of flowers. The herb-rich grassland along the upper edge of the wooded scarp supports species such as pyramidal orchid, common gromwell and basil thyme.

Most of Wenlock Edge is wooded, however, and much of it is ancient woodland, on steep slopes where there has been continuous tree cover since the end of the last Ice Age. The dominant tree is ash, but lime, yew, hazel, wych elm, field maple and others are present. Beneath the trees are found the typical shrubs of limestone soil such as spurge laurel, spindle and dogwood. The ground flora includes nettle-leaved bellflower, yellow archangel, soft shield fern, early purple orchid, common dog violet, wood sanicle, twayblade, dog's mercury and primrose.

Along the rides and in newly coppiced areas the flowers grow in more profusion and attract many butterflies. Badger and dormouse inhabit the

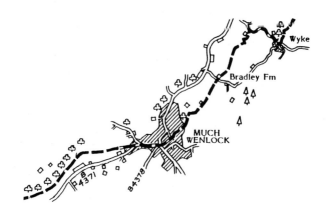

woods, while woodcock, nuthatch and spotted flycatcher are among the many species of birds to be seen. As elsewhere in Shropshire, buzzards are numerous.

Fortunately, much of Wenlock Edge is owned by the National Trust, which actively manages it for the benefit of wildlife. Conifers replaced some of the native trees in the past so the Trust is restoring broad-leaved woodland where necessary. In some areas coppicing has been reinstated, continuing a long tradition of woodland management with proven value for wildlife.

Wenlock Edge has long been seen as a valuable resource to be exploited, both for timber and for stone. Timber provided building materials, tools and charcoal for iron smelting. Limestone was used for building, for burning to produce lime, for iron smelting and, more recently, as an aggregate. This latter use still continues and there are unsightly quarries between Presthope and Much Wenlock. Throughout the woods and along the scarp are evidence of past quarrying and limestone working, much smaller in scale. Limekilns can still be seen in places.

As you enter the car park, turn left onto a descending track past a gate, and follow this as it heads into Blakeway Coppice. In spring and early summer the woodland is heady with the scent of wild garlic, and its banks bright with flowers – bugle, lesser celandine, bluebells.

You finally leave the woodland trail, on the right, at a flight of steps leading to a path rising to the top edge of the coppice. At the top of the path turn left to walk between the boundary of the coppice and a quarry.

Having passed the end of the quarry, the on-going path bears right and goes forward along the left-hand margin of a large, open field, before dipping back into the coppice at the end of Blakeway Hollow. Turn right and follow this delightful hedged track out to meet a surfaced lane, keeping forward to meet the B4371 near the Horse and Jockey pub. The hedgerow comprises a wide variety of species including viburnum, blackthorn, hazel, spindle, elder and wild rose.

Turn left and walk to a T-junction with the A458, and turn right into Much Wenlock. For safety, use a raised walkway on the left. When you reach the Gaskell Arms Hotel, a former coaching inn, have a look for the seventeenth-century squatter's cottage in Smithfield Road with its characteristic huge chimney stack (cf. Knowbury, p75). Go forward into High Street, and walk down this into the town centre.

MUCH WENLOCK TO IRONBRIDGE
Distance: 8km (5 miles)

Into my heart an air that kills
From yon far country blows;
What are those blue remembered hills,
What spires, what farms are those?

Much Wenlock

Much Wenlock is an immensely picturesque little town with a wealth of beautiful buildings in stone, brick and timber. Though small, it has a long and important history. In 1224 it was granted the right to hold a weekly market and a three-day annual fair. Edward IV granted a borough charter in 1468, giving the town jurisdiction over seventeen parishes. It even returned two MPs until 1885. Decline set in during the nineteenth century, due chiefly to the development of industry at Broseley and Ironbridge, resulting in a new regional focus of influence. The consequent lack of development was to Wenlock's benefit, resulting in the unspoilt townscape that still largely survives today.

The focus of the town is The Square, dominated by the timber-framed Guildhall, the lower part of which probably dates from 1540 and the upper from 1577. The town council still meets here every month in its upper storey. The open ground floor served as a corn market, and a live-stock market on Mondays. Close by is Holy Trinity Church, founded about 680 as a place of worship for the nuns of Wenlock Abbey. The church was enlarged between 800 and 1050 and the present nave was built around 1150 by the Cluniac monks of Wenlock Priory. There is also workmanship from several later centuries.

Other notable buildings include St Owen's Well House, the Corn Exchange, Raynalds' Mansion and Ashfield Hall, built on the site of St John's Hospital, a thirteenth-century refuge for 'lost and naked beggars'. It has also served as an inn and Charles I stayed there when on his way from Shrewsbury to Oxford during the Civil War. In many ways, how-ever, Wenlock's greatest appeal lies not in individual buildings but in its unpretentious and harmonious mix of materials and styles, and in the wealth of small but enjoyable details (old street signs, for instance) which are apparent everywhere. One particularly appealing feature is the presence of a real working farm in the town centre – Brookhouse Farm, which is of medieval origin and is to be found on the corner of Queen Street.

The most important building is just outside the town centre. This is Wenlock Priory, an English Heritage property, which is in ruins today, but was once a prosperous and powerful religious centre and a place of pilgrimage. It is thought that the name Wenlock may be from the Welsh gwyn-loc – meaning 'white monastery'. Even now, it is an inspiring place to visit, the priory church still dominating the scene with its towering gable.

The Norman chapter house has some superb decorative arcading. The ruins are those of a Cluniac priory built in the twelfth and thirteenth centuries, but Merewalh, the son of King Penda of Mercia founded the original religious house on this site, during the seventh century. He placed his daughter Milburgha in charge as Abbess in 682AD. Under her guidance the foundation flourished and she was credited with miraculous works.

Milburgha's original foundation was damaged or destroyed, possibly by a Danish raiding party, but many years later Earl Leofric of Mercia (the husband of Lady Godiva) built another religious house on the same site, which was in turn succeeded by a Cluniac one founded by Roger de

Wenlock Priory

Montgomery. Milburgha's abbey was refounded as a priory and the remains in existence today were mainly the work of Prior Humbert in the early thirteenth century.

Milburgha was originally buried in Holy Trinity Church but in 1101 her bones were removed to the newly built Priory and over the years many pilgrims came to worship at her shrine. A well bearing her name is still to be found in the town and people used to believe its water would cure eye diseases.

At the end of the High Street, turn left in front of the Guildhall into Wilmore Street. Go past Holy Trinity Church and turn right into the Bull Ring. Note the Old Savings Bank on the corner, which carries the date 1829. Continue down the lane to go past Wenlock Priory. Beyond the priory keep following a surfaced lane, and when it bends to the right, descend with it. The lane ceases to be surfaced and becomes a rough, stony track.

At Downs Mill pass to the right of a couple of houses, on a fenced path to a stile, and on to cross a brook. On the other side go left in the ensuing field. Beyond the next stile, keep on along the left

95

margin of an arable field. At the far side of the field, keep on towards Bradley Farm on a rutted track.

Just opposite Bradley Farm you reach a lane. Cross it into the farmyard, and go left to pass between buildings and walk on to a track junction. Here cross a stile a few steps to the right, and immediately go left through undergrowth to another stile into a large open pasture.

Over the stile go half-left across a large pasture, aiming for the far corner. A stile in the corner gives into another large field. Go forward alongside a well-established hedgerow. Keep following the field margin until you can branch right, half-way along it, to go to a metal gate. Beyond lies another arable field, and here the landowner has re-routed the Way around the field margin, going left until you come out onto a rough track near Woodhouse Farm. This, however, is not a lawful diversion: the correct line (often cropped over) runs across the field before turning left to reach the rough track.

Follow this to an access track, and turn right, descending into woodland, Acklands Coppice. When you reach a surfaced lane turn right and keep following the lane.

In places woodland crowds in on this quiet road on both sides. There are deer in the woods and they often venture out to graze by the edges of the lane – go quietly if you hope to see them. When the trees thin out Tickwood Hall comes into view, a splendid brick house in a fine setting, though the overall effect is rather spoilt by the intrusion of Buildwas Power Station. In front of the hall is a field, known as Audience Meadow since 1642 when Charles I met local landowners there to ask for financial help.

Just past a squatter's cottage on the right-hand side, the road bends left at a junction at Wyke. Go left along it, and about 80m/yds later leave the road and turn left, descending on a vehicle track to Vineyards Farm.

Go past Vineyards, over a stile and across the next field to another stile. Cross the top edge of the next field. On the far side, cross another stile and go forward on a path into mixed woodland, with a large number of lime trees, beech, hazel, ash, holly and birch. The path reaches a much broader track at a hairpin bend. Branch

opposite/...Titterstone Clee Hill

The world's first iron bridge, with Benthall Edge Wood in the background.
The summit of The Wrekin

right here, ascending onto Benthall Edge.

[NOTE: The original line of the Shropshire Way branches left here, not right, and takes a lower and more direct route through the woods.]

Benthall Edge is usually considered to be the final fling of Wenlock Edge before the abrupt drop into the Severn Gorge. Benthall Edge Wood is a lovely place, a real jungly tangle of trees, shrubs and ferns, and you'd never guess, on a superficial acquaintance, that this was once the scene of frenetic industry. Only the hummocky nature of the ground, and the presence of deep pits which can only be old quarries, provide any obvious clues to its past. In fact, Benthall Edge Wood was mined and quarried from the thirteenth century onwards, and especially in the eighteenth and nineteenth.

Ultimately, it was almost cleared of trees, and it's encouraging to think that today's woodland has regenerated in such a short time. Apart from the mining of coal and clay and the quarrying of limestone, the coppicing of hazel and other trees took place to provide small timber for the production of charcoal as fuel. There were brickworks, forges and wharves below by the river bank, long before the railway was built there.

Today, like most of the woods around the gorge, Benthall Edge Wood is managed by the Severn Gorge Countryside Trust, a consortium of local authorities and conservation groups. The woods are managed for the benefit of wildlife but also with public access very much in mind.

Benthall Edge Wood has enormous variety thanks to differing soil types at the east and west ends. In the east the underlying coal measures give heavy, acid soils. Oak, birch and bilberry flourish here, with alder in the damper hollows. In the west, well-drained, alkaline soils above Wenlock limestone have been brought to the surface by faulting. The limestone has produced a more varied range of vegetation, with yew, ash, beech, spindle, dogwood and a rich ground flora. Lots of mammals occur throughout the wood, including fallow deer and badgers.

The path ascends to a gate and stile, beyond which it continues for 40m/yds before making an acute left turn onto another track. At an isolated cottage bear left, back into Benthall Edge Wood. When the path forks, branch left again, and follow it round to join another one. Bear right, and when it next forks, branch left, then at the next fork, descend left, and eventually go down a flight of steps on the left.

The descending steps bring you to a path junction, where you turn right on a path signposted to Ironbridge. After crossing a delightful terraced path amid splendid mixed woodland it goes down steps, from the base of which you can move left onto the trackbed of the former Severn Valley Railway. The original course of the Shropshire Way doesn't do this, however, but goes forward to pass beneath the trackbed a few strides further on, and then turns right onto a rough-surfaced lane that leads past cottages out to meet the road at the Iron Bridge.

The trackbed technically is not a right of way but it runs through land managed by the Severn Gorge Countryside Trust, and is a more direct and easier option.

The trackbed ends at a road. Turn left and cross the Iron Bridge into the town.

Ironbridge from the Iron Bridge

SECTION 3: IRONBRIDGE TO SHREWSBURY

Between Shrewsbury and the former industrial centres of Ironbridge and Coalbrookdale, the Way delights in the pastoral landscapes of north Shropshire. Any notion that what remains is simply a 'mopping up' exercise should be instantly dispelled because, although the walking is of the easiest kind, the countryside abounds in its own pleasures that are not to be discounted. Flowers there are in plenty, while here you are more likely to see wildlife not widely encountered elsewhere along the Way – notably hare, fallow deer and fox.

To begin with there is the Wrekin, a modest height, true, but one with a commanding position that repays the effort of ascent with a stunning panorama. Beyond lies a series of charming villages and hamlets, each with its own special interest and unique place in the social history of the county.

At Wem, the journey reaches the northernmost point of the main, circular route, there turning south through Clive parish to Grinshill, where building stone has been quarried since Roman times. Beyond that easy walking leads down through Hadnall and Astley to Haughmond Abbey. At Uffington, which is associated with Wilfred Owen, the First World War poet, the River Severn is encountered for the last time, guiding the Way through to its conclusion.

IRONBRIDGE TO HIGH ERCALL
Distance: 26.3km (16½ miles)

The Severn Gorge has a long industrial history because of the availability of coal, iron ore, limestone and timber and the proximity of the River Severn for transport. The Buildwas monks were smelting iron in charcoal forges as early as 1200 and iron was made at Coalbrookdale from at least 1500. But here, as everywhere else, the fact that the smelting of iron was dependent on timber limited production. The timber had to be made into charcoal first and this was a slow process.

What changed all that was the discovery by Abraham Darby in 1709 that coke could be used for smelting. Darby's momentous discovery occurred at Coalbrookdale and sparked a revolution which changed the world. Suddenly, iron could be cheaply produced in large quantities, and it was Darby's grandson, Abraham III, who constructed the world's first iron bridge. Cast in 1779, it still spans the Severn just south of Coalbrookdale. The construction of the iron bridge led to an increasing use of iron in many areas of engineering. It proved itself in 1795 when storms and flooding damaged every local bridge except the iron one.

The whole area became heavily industrial, only to decline eventually in the face of competition from the Black Country and South Wales. For a time, however, it was the most important iron making area in the world and was celebrated for its innovations: not only the first iron bridge, but also the first iron boat, the first iron rails, the first steam locomotive.

Most of the industrial scars have now healed and the Severn Gorge is green once more, but since the 1960s those industrial relics which do survive have been transformed by the Ironbridge Gorge Museum Trust into a collection of museums which usually prove fascinating even to those who are normally bored by museums. It would be impossible to see everything in a single day so you can buy a 'passport' which is valid for one visit to each museum and lasts for an indefinite period. The Ironbridge Gorge is now a UNESCO World Heritage Site, and one of the first to be designated.

Ironbridge itself is built of mellow brick, with attractive buildings clinging in tiers to the north side of the gorge, overlooking the river. Though it has become a major tourist centre it has not lost its charm and you can soon escape the crowds by wandering along the steep, narrow streets or through the woodland well above the congested river frontage. The actual Iron Bridge is a graceful structure and the focal point of the little town. Closed to traffic since 1934, it is open to pedestrians and there's an information centre in the tollhouse on the south side of the river.

As well as Britain's best-known industrial monument, the Gorge has also produced a few famous names. Billy Wright, who captained England in the 1950s, learnt his footballing skills on the streets of Ironbridge as a child. On Church Hill, a Victorian house called The Orchard was once the home of Captain Matthew Webb (a relative of Mary Webb's husband, Henry) who was born in nearby Dawley. He learnt to swim in the Severn and in 1875 became the first man to swim the English Channel. Also born in Dawley was Edith Pargeter who, under the pseudonym Ellis Peters, has become world-famous for her Cadfael novels, set in and around Shrewsbury.

There are a number of ways from the main street in Ironbridge up to Church Hill, which is the route favoured by the Way as it heads north for Coalbrookdale. Most are narrow alleyways or flights of steps (there are steps just to the right of the Tontine Hotel, for example), and they provide a minor variation as well as the opportunity to further explore this fascinating town.

From the Iron Bridge turn right and walk along the main road as far as a roundabout, and there turn left at the foot of Church Hill. Walk all the way up Church Hill, passing the church of St Luke on the way.

At the top of Church Hill turn right onto another lane, and walk past a road junction on the right. Just at the next turning, on the left, double back left on a gravel track (signposted to Limeburners) for about 60m/yds, and then turn right into undergrowth at a footpath sign.

Follow a path until you reach a junction and turn (signposted to the Rotunda) onto wooded Lincoln Hill.

The paths through the wood, Dale Coppice, were designed by ironmaster Richard Reynolds, the son-in-law of Abraham Darby II, as 'Sabbath Walks' to provide healthy Sunday recreation for his workers. A rotunda was erected at one viewpoint, with its roof supported on cast iron columns. It became unstable and had to be demolished in 1804, so that only the foundation remains today, beneath a wooden platform built on top. From it you can see the remains of a great quarry which ate deep into Lincoln Hill. It extends so far underground that tours of its limestone caverns were enormously popular with tourists in the nineteenth century. Bands played in the illuminated caverns and thousands came on excursion trains from the Black Country and Birmingham.

Follow the on-going path through mixed woodland of beech, hawthorn and holly. Continue through the woodland with excellent views from the remains of the rotunda over the Ironbridge Gorge. At the rotunda, fences herd you round to a descending flight of steps. At the bottom turn right, and a few strides further, branch left, still descending more steps.

At the base of these pass to the right of a wall and cross a stile. Follow a path through more woodland that brings you out into a gravelled area in front of cottages. Keep forward to re-enter woodland at a stile and walk along a rising path to meet another, continuing in the same direction until you meet a signpost. Go left here, signposted to Paradise, descending steps that are slippery when wet.

The path brings you out at a surfaced lane junction. Go ahead down a narrow lane to a T-junction, and turn right at the bottom to reach the Coalbrookdale youth hostel.

Coalbrookdale was known for its coal long before the Industrial Revolution but that is not the reason for its name. In 1250 it was documented as Caldebrok, i.e. 'Coldbrook' and only its later history led people to believe this had anything to do with coal.

Just beyond the youth hostel is Holy Trinity Church, built in 1850-4 and overlooking the village, the foundries and the gorge. It was built with money given by Abraham Darby IV on his conversion to Anglicanism from Quakerism. He and his wife are buried in the churchyard and there is also a memorial to Captain Webb. Another plaque inside commemorates Thomas Parker, born in the dale in 1843, who was responsible for the first electric tramway and underground railway.

The Museum of Iron relates the story of iron from the earliest days but with special reference to the local ironmasters. It includes the Darby Furnace where in 1709 Abraham Darby I pioneered the technique of smelting iron ore with coke, thus setting in motion the sequence of events which became the Industrial Revolution. The neighbouring Coalbrookdale Works still functions as part of the Glynwed Foundries group, making Aga and Rayburn cookers. The power of steam was harnessed to iron-making here in 1742 and by 1851 the foundry was the largest in the world.

Walk past the hostel to the main road and follow this until you can branch left as if heading for the Museum of Iron. Go past the buildings that house the museum and follow the road beneath a viaduct, turning right and walking on to another junction.

The viaduct was opened in 1864, and the railway is used daily by heavy coal trains fuelling Buildwas Power Station.

Turn left at the junction and, if time allows, walk up a ramped pathway on the left that takes you to the Darby Houses.

The Darby family may have been wealthy but they needed to be close to the works to deal with any crisis which might arise so they built their fine houses just a short distance away. Rosehill was built in the 1720s for Abraham I's son-in-law. It has been carefully restored and furnished with items that belonged to the family. Next door, Dale House was built a few years earlier for Abraham I, though he died before its completion in 1717.

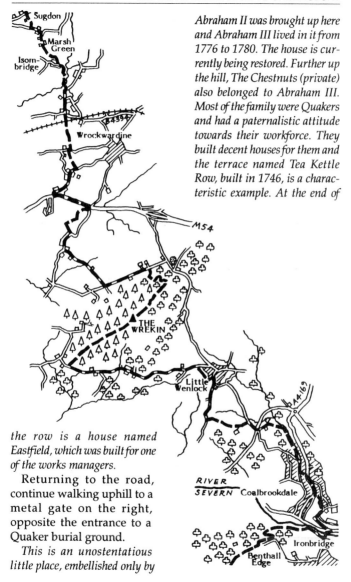

Abraham II was brought up here and Abraham III lived in it from 1776 to 1780. The house is currently being restored. Further up the hill, The Chestnuts (private) also belonged to Abraham III. Most of the family were Quakers and had a paternalistic attitude towards their workforce. They built decent houses for them and the terrace named Tea Kettle Row, built in 1746, is a characteristic example. At the end of the row is a house named Eastfield, which was built for one of the works managers.

Returning to the road, continue walking uphill to a metal gate on the right, opposite the entrance to a Quaker burial ground.

This is an unostentatious little place, embellished only by

103

some rather sombre pine trees. Simple memorials to local Quakers lean against two of the enclosing walls, with those to the Darby family on the left towards the top end. The land was bestowed by Abraham Darby II and his was the first burial though the graves themselves are unmarked.

Through the gate the on-going track is known as the Rope Walk, and it takes you past a lovely hay meadow.

This open meadow is an example of the sort of grassland that is being fertilised and 'improved' out of existence. Very few remain today, making this one all the more valuable. It is managed in the traditional way and supports a good range of plants, but is at its best in early summer when it gives a spectacular display of common spotted orchids. At one time, however, it was used by workers stretching and twisting great lengths of hemp into rope strong enough to pull cages up and down mine shafts – hence the name Rope Walk.

The Rope Walk runs above Loamhole Brook, which has formed a steep, wooded dingle cutting deeply into the Coal Measures rocks at the head of Coalbrookdale. At the southern end of the dingle is Upper Furnace Pool, which powered the bellows that blew the furnace at which Abraham Darby first smelted iron with coke. Apart from its historic interest, it has also been designated a Site of Special Scientific Interest (SSSI) for its natural history. If you would like to explore further there is access from the Rope Walk to a streamside path, mostly boardwalk, which allows a close look at the plants that flourish in the dingle, which is owned by the Severn Gorge Countryside Trust.

The pool itself is surrounded by marshy vegetation, dense and wet. The area of open water has been reduced by the invasion of a variety of aquatic plants, including marsh horsetail. Interestingly, this rather primeval-looking species is the evolutionary successor to the giant tree-like horsetails that were a major element in the swamp vegetation that 300 million years ago formed the Coal Measures.

Keep on to a stile at the entrance to Lydebrook Dingle (another SSSI). A path climbs steeply for a short while before bearing left and levelling. When it rises to a path junction, turn left and walk up to a stile at the boundary of the woodland. Go into an open pasture and head towards white gates to the left of Leasows Farm ahead. Through the gates turn left on a surfaced access, and walk out until you can turn right over a bridge spanning a road.

After about 200m/yds turn left onto a rough access track that leads to The Moors Farm. Just as you reach the farm go through a gap on the right, and turn left round two field edges, heading for a couple of radio masts in the distance. [The route around the field edges is not the lawful right of way, which cuts diagonally left across the field, and has been re-routed by the landowner.]

Cross a stile between the masts, with the Wrekin now fully in view ahead.

Go forward along the left edge of the next field until you can descend left through light woodland cover to find a terraced path bearing right to a gate and stile giving onto Buildwas Lane. Turn right up the lane, rough and stony but improving as it heads for the village of Little Wenlock.

Little Wenlock seems to have been a daughter settlement of Much Wenlock, established by the Abbey. In some ways it was a curious choice, as it is one of the highest villages in Shropshire and often gets cut off in severe weather. For most of its existence it has been dependent on opencast mining for its livelihood. Coal has been mined here since at least the beginning of the sixteenth century and was transported to iron foundries in Shirlett Forest. At the beginning of the eighteenth century Abraham Darby I laid a wooden tramway to transport coal down to his works in Coalbrookdale. This was succeeded, probably in 1767, by an iron tramway known as the ginny rail, which is believed to have been the first to be built with cast iron rails. Mining no longer plays a significant part in the village economy, but some people are still able to dig up enough coal in their gardens to fuel their fires. A plant for washing opencast coal for use in industry has been installed at Coalmoor just outside the village.

The church of St Lawrence stands on a mound in the village centre and is partly twelfth-century. The tower was built in 1667 and in 1865 a red-brick nave and chancel were added and the tower enlarged. There are few other buildings of interest in the village, except the Old Hall which is Elizabethan.

Go up to the church and turn left directly opposite into Witchwell Lane. About 100m/yds on, follow the lane, now a gravel track, as it bears right and goes past Glebelands to become a grassy track. Beyond a stile walk along a hedgeway with a splendid view left to the Stretton Hills, Long Mynd and Stiperstones. At the next stile go down to the far bottom corner of a field, and then along the right field margin that follows to another gate before walking out to meet Spout Lane.

[Walkers preferring to continue through the village should walk past the church and up to the Huntsman pub, there turning left and left again into Spout Lane, rejoining the original route near Holly Cottage.]

Turn left along Spout Lane, and follow it for 3km (2 miles) until you can leave it, on the right, at a gate giving onto a path rising through Littlehill Plantation and onto the steep south-western slopes of the Wrekin.

Shropshire's best known hill has given rise to phrases such as 'going all around the Wrekin' to describe a loquacious talker and the local toast 'to all friends around the Wrekin'. It is visible from much of Shropshire (and neighbouring counties) and is often described as the spiritual home of all true Salopians, a sort of focal point and symbol of their home county.

The Wrekin stands in splendid isolation, seeming higher than its modest 407m/1,334ft. Its shape makes people think it's an extinct volcano. It isn't, but it is volcanic in origin, a plug of worn-down rock, just a remnant of a vast chunk thrust to the surface by subterranean volcanic activity some 600 to 800 million years ago. That puts it among the oldest rocks in the world.

If that's too mundane a story, folklore provides an alternative explanation for the Wrekin. It seems that the Devil (or, in another version, a giant named Gwendol Wrekin ap Shenkin ap Mynyddmawr) had decided to damn the Severn and so flood Shrewsbury and he was on his way there with a great shovelful of soil. Meeting a cobbler with a sackful of shoes collected for repair he asks the way to Shrewsbury. The cobbler, guessing his purpose, tells him that he has already worn out all the shoes in the bag trying to find the town. Frustrated, the Devil dumps his shovelful, thus creating the Wrekin.

The top of the Wrekin is bare, but its flanks are clothed with woodland, including some fine beechwoods on the western side. Much of that belongs to Lord Barnard's Raby Estate, while the eastern side belongs to Lord Forrester of Willey Hall near Broseley. There is a Rifle Range on the north-west slopes which has been used since the First World War to provide target practice for soldiers. Warning notices are posted but do take care on firing days.

The upward route is never in doubt as it climbs to a small clearing at the top of Little Hill. From there the path descends for a while before resuming its upward flight.

As you climb, so the view (especially to the south) improves, passing over the Buildwas Power Station set against the backdrop of Benthall

Edge Wood, and extending southwards as far as the Malvern Hills, the Forest of Dean and the Cotswolds.

Eventually the ascending path breaks free of the trees and runs along the crest to the summit trig pillar.

On a clear day one of the most stunning panoramas in the Midlands is revealed. The view to the west includes Earl's Hill, Long Mountain, the Breiddens and the Berwyns. To the east lie Telford, the Black Country and Cannock Chase, while to the north the meres and mosses of the plain are punctuated by sandstone outcrops such as Haughmond Hill, Hawkstone and Grinshill before Shropshire merges seamlessly into Cheshire. To the south, of course, lie all the hills with which you have already become familiar, and the top of the Wrekin is one place from which you can really appreciate the contrast between the landscapes of north and south Shropshire. It's also one of the few places from which you can trace the course of the River Severn in a way not possible elsewhere.

This view was also important, though for different reasons, to the Celtic people who colonised the Severn Valley from the seventh century BC. They seem to have gradually established control over neighbouring tribes

The Wrekin from the Shropshire Way at Aston

and they chose the Wrekin for their 'capital'. They built a substantial hill-fort on top and excavation has revealed evidence of timber palisading and hut circles. The Romans, who called these people the Cornovii, subdued them and sacked the fort, establishing their own camp at nearby Wroxeter, which they called Viroconium Cornovirum. The Cornovii were gradually assimilated and many settled at Viroconium, which grew into a large town.

The ramparts of the fort are still in evidence on the Wrekin, and the two northern entrances have been named Heaven Gate and Hell Gate. There are also some craggy outcroppings of former volcanic lavas, the largest of which, to the south of the summit, is known as the Needle's Eye. It's a cleft rock, which has given rise to the story that it was split in two at the instant of the Crucifixion.

Cross the summit and continue on the other side, descending a broad trail that goes via Heaven Gate and Hell Gate down into woodland, with prominent 'Danger Area' signs on your left. Lower down, when the track forks, branch left, and when it bends sharply to the right, leave it and turn left at a prominent beech tree. Continue descending pleasantly through extensive woodland until, just after some limekilns set back on the right, the track bends right. A few strides on, now near the bottom edge of the woodland, leave the track on an indistinct path through an adjacent hedgerow and go forward across an arable field to a stile giving onto a lane (Wrekin Course).

Turn left for 1km (half a mile), and then go right to follow a quiet lane as far as a T-junction at Aston Hall Farm. Turn right again and walk up to Aston Farm, finally leaving the road as you reach the last buildings by branching left onto a farm track. Follow this up to meet a hedgerow.

Turn right alongside the hedge until, just before a hedge corner, you can pass through a gap in it. Stay beside the hedge for a few strides, and then bear half-left to the far corner of a pasture (near an advertisement hoarding). After a stile walk down the edge of the next field, parallel with the busy A5, to a stile near the foot of a bridge embankment. Turn right to another stile, and then go left up steps to the road. Turn left, over the A5 bridge, and at the junction ahead turn left onto the B5061 for about 800m/yds.

At Overley leave the B-road, turning right for Leaton. Just as you approach the entrance to a quarry branch left on a side road.

Follow this through Leaton and, just after the last houses on the right, leave the lane, going left at a signpost into an arable field. Go across to an electricity pylon, and keep on to a stile concealed in a hedgerow. Cross the next field in the same direction to meet a lane near Tiddicross Stables.

Turn right for 60m/yds, and then leave the lane, on the left, over a stile. Go around the right-hand edge of the ensuing paddock until a stile gives access to an arable field. Turn left alongside a hedge, and when this turns away, keep on in the same direction towards an isolated oak tree in mid-field. Carry on to cross a railway line.

Gradually now the Wrekin slips away behind you as you go forward into the pastoral landscapes of north Shropshire, heading for the town of Wem, and the most northerly point of the Way.

Beyond the railway, walk forward across the next field to the Plough Inn at Cross Green. Go down the lane opposite into Allscott.

Once part of the huge manor of Wrockwardine, this is a pleasant village with an attractive Georgian manor house, but, like the surrounding countryside, it does tend to be dominated by the huge sugar beet factory just to the west.

After about 500m/yds, turn left at Mill House onto a gravel track to Allscott Mill. Go forward into a garden, and keep to the right of the buildings to locate a footbridge spanning the River Tern. Beyond the bridge, follow the riverbank.

This brief flirtation with the River Tern, little more than 300m/yds, is quite delightful, and it is not unusual, in addition to the normal river birds like mallard and moorhen, to see the occasional kingfisher, and skeins of Canada geese overhead. The banks of the river in summer are bright with ragwort, forget-me-not and purple loosestrife. During late July and August you may find the ragwort festooned with the striped caterpillars of the cinnabar moth (Tyria jacobeae), a day-flying moth often mistaken for a butterfly. Much as the caterpillars may love ragwort, it is, nevertheless, highly toxic to farm animals.

Eventually, as the river bends right, bear left to Isombridge Farm.

The tiny, remote hamlet of Isombridge stands by the River Tern and there is no River Isom so it's a rather puzzling name. In fact, the original form was Esnebrugg, which means 'Bridge of the Servant'. The only bridge today is the bridleway one on which the Shropshire Way crosses the Tern at Allscott.

Pass through a gate and go to the right of farm buildings to a lane. Turn right, then take the first turning on the left and follow the lane through Marsh Green, and up to a T-junction at Sugdon.

Go forward onto a green lane, following this round until you meet a farm track, and then turn right, passing the entrance to Sugdon Farm. When the track turns into a field, leave it by going right over a stile. Walk beside the on-going hedgerow to a gap next to a large oak tree. Turn left, and walk on to meet a surfaced farm track. Turn right along the track until you cross a cattle grid, and there go immediately left over a stile.

Head for a stile in the far corner, near a sewage treatment plant, and then walk around the edges of two pastures until you meet a double metal gate at a lane. Cross the lane and go through the gate opposite to access an enclosed pathway at the rear of properties. Follow this until it ends near the church of St Michael and All Angels in High Ercall, and there turn left along Church Road, walking out to meet the village road.

High Ercall is basically an attractive village, but one which suffers from its position at a busy road junction. There are some interesting old buildings, including Ercall Hall, the church, the Toll House and some almshouses founded by the Earl of Bradford in 1694. Ercall Hall was built in 1608 on the site of the Manor House by Sir Francis Newport, an officer in Charles I's army. It was later fortified and garrisoned in the Civil War, holding out against a siege for a year before the Royalists surrendered in 1646. In fact, High Ercall was, along with Ludlow, the last Shropshire garrison to hold out for the King. The curious arcade of four arches visible in the garden at the rear of the Hall is probably part of the original Manor House built by the de Arkles, the family after whom the village is named.

The eleventh-century church of St Michael was damaged in the Civil War and shot marks can still be seen on the walls. It was restored in 1865 by Street. Nearby is the Gospel Oak, under which Methodist religious meetings were once held.

HIGH ERCALL TO STANTON UPON HINE HEATH
Distance: 11.3km (7 miles)

Leave High Ercall along Park Lane, opposite the end of Church

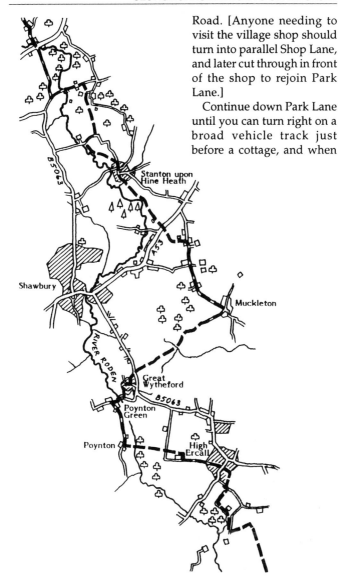

Road. [Anyone needing to visit the village shop should turn into parallel Shop Lane, and later cut through in front of the shop to rejoin Park Lane.]

Continue down Park Lane until you can turn right on a broad vehicle track just before a cottage, and when

111

this turns right into a field, leave it, by going left alongside a hedgerow. When you reach a hedge corner, keep forward across the next field (ignoring a waymark suggesting that you should go left along a field boundary – the correct right of way keeps straight ahead here). Cross a concrete farm track, and keep on in the same direction.

On the far side of the field, go through a hedgerow, and forward, descending, to cross the River Roden by a footbridge. Go up the next field, aiming for a stile to the right of a gate, and so reach Poynton directly opposite the scant remains of an old chapel incorporated into a wall of a farm building. A three-light Perpendicular window and part of the medieval west wall are all that survive.

Turn right and walk along the lane to Poynton Green, and there turn right for Great Wytheford.

The manor of Great Wytheford has a long and complicated history, having changed hands several times after the Conquest, with part of it originally going to the Sheriff and the rest to William Pantulf, who built the castle at Wem. In the thirteenth century it went to the FitzAlans, patrons of Haughmond Abbey. At the time of Domesday there was a mill on the River Roden and later there was a forge, where iron was worked.

Today, the attractive Forge Cottage by the river probably stands on the same site. Behind the cottage is imposing Wytheford Hall, part of such a substantial farming community that it is virtually a hamlet in its own right. A little further on, Little Wytheford is another impressive house.

Just having crossed the River Roden again, turn left on a gravel track running beside a house to locate a stile at the rear. Cross a brook, and in the next field head for the top corner. Beyond follow the right-hand field boundary to walk out to a farm track. Turn right to a surfaced lane. Turn left, and when you emerge on the B5063, cross it and go forward onto a broad farm track heading out across a prairie-like field.

When the track bears right, leave it, on the left, to strike across fields that are often cropped over. Aim for a stag-headed oak (i.e. a tree with bare branches protruding above its leafy canopy) in a hedgerow in the far distance, beyond which you cross the next two fields to the corner of light woodland. On the far side of the field you come onto a broad farm track. Turn right along this, and follow it out to meet a road just past Muckleton Hall Farm.

Turn left and continue along the road for about 2km (1¼ miles), passing the junction with Muckleton Road, and then leave it immediately after an isolated house on the left, turning left onto a rough driveway.

Pass to the left of a house and stables, and go forward onto a broad grassy path, heading for a barn-like building. Just before reaching it, go left over a stile, and along the right-hand edge of the ensuing field. Enter a large arable field by a stile adjoining an oak tree, and strike across the field, aiming to the right of a line of tall poplars in the distance, beyond the A53.

Cross the road and go down the access opposite to Sowbath Farm. As you reach the farm buildings, go through the farmyard compound and on to reach a metal gate beyond. Through this cross the next field, continuing in much the same direction to the far left corner.

Concealed from view until the last moment, a gate allows you to cross a feeder of the nearby River Roden, and then to go forward alongside the plantation that flanks the river, and (in so doing) along the edge of two fields. From a stile to the right of a gate, go alongside a post and wire fence with the village (and church) of Stanton upon Hine Heath coming into view ahead.

Over the next stile turn right along the field edge. At the end of a hedgerow, cross a small field to reach the end of Church Lane. Walk up into the village.

Like so many in Shropshire, Stanton upon Hine Heath is a pleasant but unremarkable village. There are some attractive old houses and St Andrew's Church has a Norman nave and chancel and some herring-bone masonry in the north wall – a rare feature and one that always indicates either Saxon or very early Norman workmanship. The thir-teenth-century tower is topped with fifteenth-century pinnacles and supported by heavy buttresses dated 1666. The church sits on a roughly circular mound, suggesting a possible pre-Christian origin for this site of worship. Tucked away to the north of the village is Harcourt Manor, formerly called The Woodlands, where the young Mary Webb lived from 1896 to 1902.

STANTON UPON HINE HEATH TO WEM
Distance: 9.6km (6 miles)

At the top of Church Lane as you come into Stanton, with the church of St Andrew off to your left, go briefly into Church Road and then immediately left. Keep forward to a road junction and then out along the road for Moreton Corbett and Wem. There is a post office, shop and pub in Stanton for anyone who needs them.

When the road bends left, keep forward along a lane signposted to Harcourt Mill. After about 200m/yds go over a stile on the left, half-right across a large field to a fence corner, and then follow the fence round two field edges to a stile. In the next field, walk beside a hedgerow on your right. When you emerge on a lane, turn right, and after about 250m/yds leave it, on the left, at a double gate with stiles, to head across a field.

In the far corner cross a stile, walk past a nearby beech tree, and continue in the same direction. From a stile on the far side go immediately left through a gate and right alongside a fence to the edge of a plantation. Keep on to a brief, enclosed path through undergrowth beside buildings, emerging onto a vehicle track. Walk along it for a short distance, then, as it bends right, leave it, going forward into and then up through a small plantation. From the top stile go forward first with the plantation boundary, and later with a fence on your right to a stile in a wall. Beyond this go left on a rough lane which passes between two houses to become a green lane, passing more houses lower down before keeping on to Papermill Bridge. Here you cross the River Roden on the first of four occasions before reaching Wem.

The access runs on to meet a surfaced lane. Just as it does so, turn sharp right onto another track that soon climbs into woodland and through a sandstone cutting. Eventually you emerge at the A49, crossing with care into the road opposite and recrossing the Roden as you enter Lee Brockhurst.

Lee Brockhurst is an attractive place sheltering at the foot of the wooded slopes of Lee Hill, which is owned by the National Trust. The name means 'a clearing in a badger wood' or 'under a badger hill'. It was once of some strategic importance, lying by the main Shrewsbury to Whitchurch road with an old bridge over the River Roden. The present bridge was built in

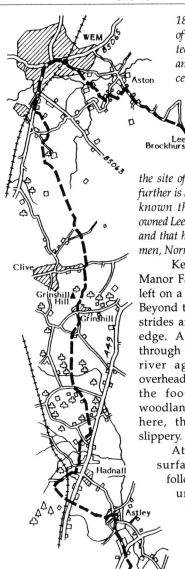

1800 to Telford's design. Some of the houses date from the fifteenth and sixteenth centuries and St Peter's Church is twelfth-century with some later work, including Victorian additions. Across the road from the church is a low mound upon which a barn has been erected. The mound is the site of an early castle but nothing further is known about it, although it is known that Roger de Montgomery owned Lee Brockhurst after the Conquest and that he gave it to one of his huntsmen, Norman Venator.

Keep on past a chapel and Manor Farm until you can branch left on a dirt track to a metal gate. Beyond the gate go forward a few strides and then left down a field edge. At the bottom go ahead through undergrowth to cross the river again, and then use an overhead power line to guide you to the foot of steps rising into woodland ahead. Take great care here, the steps are extremely slippery.

At the top, as you meet a surfaced lane, turn left and follow it for 1km (half a mile) until you meet a rough-surfaced vehicle track going left beside a cottage. Go along it, pass an isolated cottage, and then keep forward along a

115

path through the edge of woodland. When this emerges at Barker's Green, turn left, and shortly go right into Weir Lane.

When the lane surfacing ends, go left over a stile beside a house to a bridge spanning the Roden, and keep on across the ensuing field and up the right-hand edge of the next. When you meet a gravelled lane go forward to Aston Road. Turn left to a railway crossing, and over this keep on into the centre of Wem. Keep forward until you can turn left into Mill Street.

Wem

Wem may not be the most instantly appealing town in Shropshire, but it does have its moments. Despite the slight air of neglect that prevails, it is worth exploring for it's a traditional market town with a variety of interesting, if unspectacular, buildings. Few of them are very old, because the town was partially demolished in 1643 when a band of 40 Parliamentarians defeated an attacking force of 5,000 Royalists. Further destruction followed in 1677 when 14-year-old Jane Churm ensured herself a place in local history by accidentally setting alight the thatched roof of her home. The resulting 'Great Fire of Wem' destroyed nearly 150 buildings in less than an hour.

The church, dedicated to St Peter and St Paul, has a fourteenth-century doorway of an uncommon design, but much of the rest of the building is of the Victorian period. Next to it stands a mound which was the site of a castle built here by the Norman baron William Pantulf in the eleventh century. It was apparently a substantial structure but it gradually fell into decay, a process helped by the propensity of locals to remove its stones for other building purposes. Wem had medieval town walls too, but no trace of these survives.

A number of notable people have been born in Wem, or have lived or owned houses there – men such as essayist William Hazlitt, biographer John Ireland, portrait painter John Astley, actor William Betty and the notorious Judge Jeffreys, of 'Bloody Assize' fame. But the one whom Wem is most proud of is Henry Eckford, who in 1887 developed the modern version of that beautiful garden flower, the sweet pea.

WEM TO GRINSHILL
Distance: 6.4km (4 miles)

Continue down Mill Street and walk past the old mill with its tall
chimney.

*There has been a mill on this site for over 800 years, but the present
building dates from 1656 and was restored in 1819. It was still in use as
recently as the 1980s.*

Keep on following the road as it bends left to pass beneath a
railway line. Swing right with the main road beyond, and keep on
past a garage until, just after passing Oaklands, you can turn left
onto a broad access track, over a cattle grid, and head for
Pankeymoor Cottages, a black and white building set in trees just
ahead. Cross another cattle grid, and continuing on the broad track.

As you approach the cottages, cross a nearby stile and the
ensuing fields, passing beneath power lines, finally to pass between
two ponds and reach the lane at Tilley Green, a hamlet with a few
old cottages. Cross the lane and the stile opposite, and bear right
along the edge of a garden, keeping forward across a field towards
another cottage, just before which you reach a stile next to a gate.
Cross the stile and go forward past the cottage to a surfaced lane.

Cross the lane, a stile and a narrow field to another stile on the
edge of a large open pasture, separated from an adjacent and much
larger field by a fence, across which there is a stile. The onward
path cuts across the fields, heading to the right of Trench Hall, set
in a small mixed woodland ahead.

*Trench Hall is a fine, red-brick house with stone dressings and an
unusual double pediment at roof level.*

Eventually the path runs on to meet a stile at a hedge corner.
Cross the stile and go forward with a hedgerow on your left,
leaving the field at another stile just as the spire of Clive church
appears on the horizon ahead. Now go forward with the hedgerow
on your right along another field margin for about 500m/yds to
another stile, beyond which keep on alongside a hedgerow to reach
a rough track, over a stile.

Turn right for 200m/yds and then leave the track, on the left,
through a gate (signposted), and keep right to a stile (waymarked)
next to a pond. In the ensuing field, keep to the right-hand field

edge to a stile/gate at another lane. Cross the lane and go into the next field and then forward to the right of a pond, heading across the field in the same direction, alongside a hedgerow on the left, and aiming for a group of houses at Quarry View. Another stile, another field and then onto the lane at Quarry View, at the edge of the village of Clive.

Clive is worth the slight detour if you enjoy unspoilt villages. Its stone-built cottages cluster prettily on the slopes of Grinshill Hill around All Saints Church, whose spire is a landmark for many miles around. A Norman foundation, which was rebuilt by the Victorians, All Saints' has a steep and utterly charming churchyard that is awash with daffodils in spring. It shelters the bones of William Wycherley (1640-1716), a Restoration dramatist whose best-known work is probably 'The Country Wife' (1675). He was born at Clive Hall, an Elizabethan (or possibly earlier) manor house. Intriguingly, there is a network of tunnels under the village, the result of copper mining, which was begun here by the Romans and carried on until 1886.

Turn right, and in 20m/yds go left over another stile to follow a path along a field edge. At the end of the field, go right, through a gate, and immediately left along a hedgerow. At the top of the field cross a stile at the rear of a cottage. Go past the cottage to reach a track and turn right. Shortly, leave the track, on the left, into the woodland that cloaks Grinshill Hill.

A short way on, after passing a disused quarry on the right, branch left and descend steeply on a path that curves round and runs down to the village of Grinshill. Take great care on the descent following wet weather.

Alternatively, before branching left, follow the path that goes to the right. This will take you to the top of Grinshill Hill, the summit of which is marked by a trig pillar, a toposcope and a radar mast. To return, retrace your steps until just before the quarry and then branch right and go down towards Grinshill.

The various paths through the woodland of Grinshill Hill are confusing, but, if in doubt, keep going downhill, and eventually you will reach a path that runs into the village. As you reach the first building bear slightly right and then go left on a track leading down to All Saints' Church.

The hard sandstone ridge of Grinshill Hill is part of the discontinuous semi-circle of New Red Sandstone that outcrops here and there to enliven the north Shropshire plain. The sandstone is about 200 million years old, and was once part of a series of dunes inhabited by primitive lizard-like reptiles called rhynchosaurus, whose fossilised skeletons and footprints have occasionally been found. The ridge has been quarried since Roman times but, until the mid-nineteenth century, the stone was used only in Shropshire. Massive blocks were hauled to the River Roden to be floated down to the Tern, and ultimately the Severn, to build the twelfth-century abbey at Buildwas, as well as many churches throughout the county.

The construction of the railways, and the opening of Yorton Station in 1858, meant it could be transported much further, and buildings of Grinshill stone came to grace many a town and city. It was used for several railway stations (Shrewsbury was the first; others included Crewe, Chester, Cheltenham and Gloucester) and for many of the grandiose building projects of Victorian Britain. Lord Hill's Column in Shrewsbury contains 1,000 tons of it and is reputedly the tallest Doric column in the world. Some was even transported to America. Quarrying still continues at Grinshill today, with two types of sandstone extracted – red and white, though the latter, which is of higher quality, may actually be pink, yellow or grey.

The east end of the hill is clothed by Corbet Wood, a nature reserve given to the county council by Sir John Corbet in 1971, and graced by some particularly splendid Scots pines. Further west the land rises to the open common of the summit, where the heathy vegetation includes acid-loving grasses and flowers such as heath bedstraw and tormentil. There is a toposcope here, erected on the occasion of the Queen's Silver Jubilee in 1977. Although you're only at 192m (630ft), the view includes the Wrekin, Wenlock Edge, the Clees, the Strettons, the Long Mynd, Jodrell Bank, the Peckforton Hills, the Arans and the Berwyns.

Below the summit grows woodland that is mostly the result of natural regeneration on old quarry sites. The shallow, sandy soil favours trees such as birch and rowan and there is a ground cover of bracken and bilberry, all of which makes a delightful change from the surrounding intensively farmed landscape. Woodland songbirds think so too, and summer migrants like chiffchaff and willow warbler breed here, along with blackbird, robin and wren.

Grinshill village is a charming place that includes many examples of building work in the local stone. The houses are built in a wide variety of styles and some of them from the most enormous blocks of stone. The

119

Manor is an imposing twin-gabled house bearing the date 1624 and there is a good-looking Georgian pub, the Elephant and Castle Hotel. All Saints' Church is an endearingly odd Victorian building (1839-40) in neo-Norman with an Italian-style tower. Just east of the village, Stone Grange is a lovely building known locally as the Pest House, because it was built as a country refuge for times of plague by Shrewsbury School in 1617.

GRINSHILL TO SHREWSBURY
Distance: 19.3km (12 miles)

Go down past the church to a T-junction and turn right, shortly going left into Sandy Lane. Just as you approach a cottage on the right, leave the lane, branching right onto a short, overgrown path (signposted) to a stile. Go down the edge of two fields, and then, having crossed two stiles close together, walk across the corner of a field towards a gate, to the left of which another stile gives onto a surfaced lane.

Turn right and immediately left onto a broad field edge track. [The correct line cuts across a field to intersect a hedge and cross the next field. There is no way through the hedge at the time of writing, so the field edge track is the only option.]

At the top end of the second field follow the track round to the right until you can go left through a gate at a corner of woodland. Follow the on-going track out to meet a road near the entrance to Hardwicke Stables. Turn left for 50m/yds and then cross a stile into woodland on the right. Move towards the left edge of the woodland, and then along a path beside an iron fence to and through a kissing gate. Cross three fields, always in the same direction (making allowances for fields being cropped over). On the far side of the third field you enter woodland, and can go forward on a green path to a rough-surfaced lane at a cottage built with large sandstone blocks.

Go right for a few strides, left over a stile, and down the edge of the ensuing field. Cross another field to a stile beside a gate, and then on along an enclosed path, keeping right when you encounter a wall. This will bring you into the corner of a small field. Go along the right-hand edge to a lane. Cross the lane, and go forward into Ladymas Lane for about 100m/yds, and then branch left onto a green path to the left of a large cottage.

In the next field go towards the right-hand edge of a group of new houses, bearing right on the far side of the field to a stile beside a pond. Go through a nearby gate and across the next field to a lane. Turn left and just before Hadnall church turn right through a gate.

A large, sprawling village, Hadnall contains no buildings of outstanding interest. The church of St Mary Magdalene is partly Norman with a fourteenth-century nave but was largely rebuilt in the nineteenth century. It contains a monument to Viscount Hill (1772-1842) who fought with Wellington at Waterloo. He was a leading general throughout the Peninsular War and Commander-in-Chief of the British Army from 1828 to 1842.

Hill lived much of his life at Hardwicke Grange to the north of Hadnall. The house has been demolished, but the stables survive and are now used as industrial units. To celebrate his military exploits he built Waterloo Windmill, a replica of one near the battle site. The remains of the replica still stand close to the Shropshire Way.

[Along the main road in Hadnall there is a village stores, post-office and tourist information point. Walkers needing these facilities should continue past the church to the road and turn right, rejoining the Way at the next road on the right.]

When you reach a lane, turn right, and keep on until the lane bends right near a farm. Then leave it, on the left, over a stile, striking across a large field to a railway crossing point on the far side. Cross the railway, and the road beyond (both with great care), and go forward along a hedge to cross a narrow lane and the open field beyond, heading for an oak tree in mid-field. On the other side a stile gives access to a large arable field. Cross this, with the Stretton Hills and the Long Mynd putting in an appearance on the right.

In the field that follows go half-left to a stile in a hedgerow, forward along the left-hand edge of a meadow, and along the right-hand edge of the next field to emerge on a rough-surfaced lane. Go down this and forward to the church in Astley village.

Dedicated to St Mary, the church is basically of the fourteenth century, though some twelfth-century work survives. However, it was given a new tower in 1837 and then much restored in 1887. Nearby is the imposing, though slightly bizarre, façade of Astley House, with classical Greek architecture (Corinthian pilasters and Doric columns) adorning

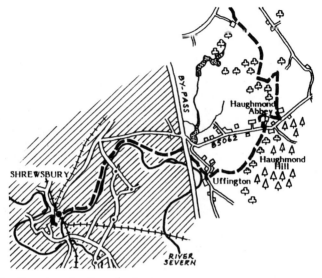

its otherwise sober Georgian frontage.

Bear right with the road in front of the church and walk on to meet a main road, near the Dog in the Lane pub at Upper Astley.

Cross the road, bearing right to gain a broad field-edge track on the left. When you reach a metal gate, follow the now enclosed track round as far as Wheatley Farm. Cross a brook just before the farm, and then a stretch of rough ground to reach the continuing lane. This guides you into a large open pasture. Go across this, along the line of a grubbed-out hedgerow of which only a couple of trees remain.

On the far side, cross a stile beside a gate and walk beside a hedgerow on your right, following this round to a farm track. Cross a stile into a large field, and keep on in the same direction to the far corner where Colins Rough (on your right) meets New Coppice (ahead).

Ignore the stile on the right, and instead turn left, following the boundary of New Coppice to a fence. Turn left alongside the fence, across two fields until you meet a metal kissing gate near Ebury Hill (the site of a prehistoric fort), at the head of a long straight farm track.

Haughmond Abbey

Turn down the track to Haughmond (pronounced Hormond) Farm, and, just after a slurry tank, go through a gate and walk out along the farm access. At the end of the access, turn right over a stile and cross a field (aiming almost due west), heading for a stile over a wall.

Over the wall pass through an area of undergrowth to meet a forest track in Abbey Wood. Turn right for a few strides until you can descend left beside a fence to walk around the perimeter of the abbey grounds, finally emerging near the entrance to the abbey. The grounds of Haughmond Abbey make an ideal place to take a breather before the final stage into Shrewsbury.

The exact origins of Haughmond Abbey are unknown, but one of the earliest surviving records dates from around 1135 and refers to 'Prior Fulk and his brethren', who were probably Augustinian canons. There is a tradition that it was founded as a hermitage and may have begun as part of the monastic reform movement at the end of the eleventh century, when small, austere communities of priests were established on comparatively isolated sites.

Early in the twelfth century it attracted the patronage of the FitzAlan family of Clun. They supported Empress Matilda in the Civil Wars of King Stephen's reign, and when her son became Henry II in 1154 the FitzAlans were well rewarded. They could afford rich endowments for Haughmond, which gained the status, unusual for an Augustinian house, of an abbey. Henry appointed his old tutor, Alfred, as Abbot and from then on Haughmond enjoyed considerable prosperity, which is reflected in its fine buildings, ranged around two courtyards cut into the hillside on a series of terraces.

Most of what survives belongs to the late twelfth century and the fourteenth century. The arches in the chapter house feature wonderful carvings of saints, including St Augustine of Hippo, St Thomas à Becket, St Catherine, St John the Evangelist, St John the Baptist, St Margaret of Antioch, St Winefred and St Michael. St Catherine is shown standing on the head of Emperor Maxentius, who had her martyred, and St Winefred stands on the head of her would-be murderer, Prince Caradog. St John the Baptist, to whom the abbey is dedicated, stands on the head of King Herod.

Look out also for a superb wooden ceiling (probably early sixteenth-century) in the chapter house, a richly decorated bay window in the abbot's private rooms and carvings of St Peter and St Paul in the cloister. In the remains of the abbey church are the tombstones of two of the abbey's patrons, John FitzAlan, who died in 1272, and his wife, Isabel de Mortimer.

The abbey was suppressed in 1539, after which the abbot's hall and the adjoining rooms were converted into a private house. After a fire during the Civil War the ruins became a working farm and there was still a cottage on the site of the kitchens when the abbey was placed in state care in 1933. It is now looked after by English Heritage, which is hoping to open a small refreshment kiosk on the site.

Walk out along the access lane to meet a road. Turn left and soon go right, over a stile beside a gate to follow a clear path across the wooded lower slopes of Haughmond Hill.

Much of the woodland clothing flat-topped Haughmond Hill is owned by the Forestry Commission, but there is an interesting mix of tree species. It is basically acidic oak woodland with ash, sycamore, holly, silver birch, rowan and beech, and with a ground cover of bracken, bramble, wood sage, foxglove, dog's mercury and enchanter's nightshade. If you pass quietly through the woodland you may be rewarded with a sighting of a few of the fallow deer that live here. A vast working quarry is also concealed in the woodland – you won't see it but you will certainly hear it if you walk through on a weekday.

Scots pines crown the rocky top, where there is also an Iron Age fort. The Romans probably had a camp on the west of the hill so they could guard the Chester road. There are tremendous views from the top and it's worth the detour, if you have the time and energy (just keep on along the southern edge of the hill until a path gives access to the top).

Keep following the path through the woodland until you reach an electricity pylon. Here, turn left through undergrowth to a stile. Beyond this, cross the next field to Brickkiln Bridge where you cross the disused Shrewsbury Canal, and may see the occasional kingfisher.

This is one of the few stretches of the old canal still to contain water. It was originally 27km (17 miles) long and was built between 1793 and 1797 to link the county town with the Wombridge Canal at Trench (near what is now Telford). There, an inclined plane lowered and raised boats to and from the coalfield plateau, which was served by a network of tub boat waterways built in the late eighteenth century.

The Shrewsbury Canal was a particularly narrow one, so much so that the barges used on it were known as 'narrer-narrer boats'. It was built largely under the supervision of Thomas Telford, who introduced some novel features, including one of the world's first iron aqueducts (which may still be seen, marooned in a field at Longdon-upon-Tern). The canal closed in 1944, since when parts of it have been deliberately filled in and other sections have naturally silted up.

Keep forward to a gate and stile and then walk out to the road, opposite the Corbett Arms. Turn right into the village of Uffington.

Uffington is a small village today, but must have been a busy place once. There was a wharf here, serving the Shrewsbury Canal, though a row of cottages is all that marks the place now. The road through the village used to cross the canal on a humpback bridge that features in a watercolour painting by Harold Owen, brother of Wilfred, the war poet. Today the canal has been infilled and the bridge has gone but the Owen connection is still remembered.

Wilfred Owen was born the son of a railway worker in Oswestry in 1893 but in 1907 the family moved to Shrewsbury. They used to enjoy walking beside the Severn, and would often cross the river to Uffington by way of the cable ferry that operated then. Sometimes they attended evensong at Holy Trinity Church, which was rebuilt in 1856 in Early

English style, though its windows contain some sixteenth- and seven-teenth-century glass from the Netherlands and Germany

When not at Uffington, the family would be on the other side of the river, where one day Wilfred noticed Harold's boots were covered in buttercup petals and described them as 'blessed with gold'. Years later, during the Great War, he used the same image when describing soldiers at the front in 'Spring Offensive'. Wilfred Owen was killed a week before the Armistice.

Walk down the road, going past Holy Trinity Church and the top of Mill Lane. Keep on to pass the Old Post Office and Wharf Cottage, and then turn left onto a footpath running through the edge of woodland.

[NOTE: The Shropshire Way is signposted down Mill Lane, from which there appears to be no escape other than by passing through someone's landscaped garden. This is a legitimate right of way, and there is no evidence that walkers have been discouraged from walking through the garden. In this instance, however, there is an alternative, as described. Both the Old Post Office and Wharf Cottage are interesting and attractive buildings, and worth the slightly longer detour.]

The on-going footpath passes beneath the A49, and rises to meet an access lane at Pimley Manor. A quick right and left take you onto a path through the Old Shrewsbury Canal Countryside Heritage Site, a sort of linear nature reserve that includes the silted-up canal. As you walk along the view opens up, giving you a first glimpse of journey's end.

Keep on to a junction of pathways (near another heritage site signpost). Ignore the Shropshire Way waymark sending you forward (this is a variant route that is available if the riverside path is flooded), and instead branch left onto a path through undergrowth. This soon brings you beside the River Severn, which will now remain your companion almost to the end of the walk.

Go beneath the A5112 and soon emerge on a wider track. Go left, alongside the river. When you reach a surfaced road, keep on beside the river. At the weir, stay with the riverside towpath.

Pass under the railway bridge, and then about 200m/yds further on, turn right up St Mary's Water Lane. At the top turn right again to the main street. Turn right, going down past the entrance to the castle, and on to finish the walk at the station.

THE SHROPSHIRE WAY (Clockwise)

In the following clockwise description of the Shropshire Way additional information on sites and scenes of particular interest and notes of historical, archaeological, sociological and other significance have been omitted. At the point in the text where they would occur a cross-reference is made to the parallel section in the main (anticlockwise) route description, either as a page number (25), or with a word or two of reference (Haughmond Abbey, 123).

SECTION 3: SHREWSBURY TO IRONBRIDGE

Setting off in a clockwise direction tackles first the delightfully easy pastoral landscapes of north Shropshire, and though much of this section is without noticeable gradient, there are still a few moments, as on the ascent of Grinshill Hill, when effort is required. In the northern part of the walk, too, footpaths are generally less well walked, and, as a result, at certain times of the year it is not unusual to find paths overgrown (shorts wearers should bear this in mind).

The scenery, however, is always most agreeable, and there are few moments when the silhouettes of higher ground - the Wrekin, the Stretton Hills, Long Mynd, Brown Clee Hill and Stiperstones - are not present on the southern horizon.

Between Shrewsbury and Ironbridge there are few towns and villages at which supplies can be obtained. The first is Wem, though there is a pub in Grinshill, but then it is Stanton upon Hine Heath and High Ercall before you encounter another shop along the route. Beyond High Ercall there is nothing between you and Ironbridge. So, be sure you're well provisioned.

SHREWSBURY TO GRINSHILL
Distance: 19.3km (12 miles)

(Shrewsbury, 22) From the station walk up past the castle entrance and then, opposite Woolworths, turn left into Windsor Place (signposted to the river), and then take the next left, descending

St Mary's Water Lane. At the bottom of the lane you reach the River Severn and turn left on a riverside path.

Keep beside the river, passing a weir along the way, and then walking either on a road or the verge beside it until the road bends left. When it does, leave it and take to a riverside footpath. When you reach the bridge carrying the A5112, branch right and go beneath the bridge. The path eventually rises to a path junction on the edge of Heathgates, where you enter the Old Shrewsbury Canal Countryside Heritage Site (Old Shrewsbury Canal, 125). Turn right, following a broad path beside the old canal, both of which gradually move away from the river.

The canalside track ends at a lane giving access to Pimley Manor. Continue on the other side of the lane to pass below the A49. Follow the on-going path out to meet a road at the northern edge of Uffington (125).

[NOTE: Before reaching the road, the Shropshire Way officially goes right, over a stile, across a field, and then forward through private landscaped gardens to finish up Mill Lane beside the church. This is the correct route, and there has been no evidence that the householders have objected to walkers going through their garden. Our variant takes you past some interesting old buildings associated with the Shrewsbury Canal.]

Turn right into the village and go past Holy Trinity Church for about 150m/yds, and then leave the road by turning left onto a gravel track directly opposite the Corbett Arms.

Go into a field and across the top of it, crossing the course of the old Shrewsbury Canal once more at Brickkiln Bridge, and then go forward to a stile. Beyond this you enter a narrow neck of woodland. Walk to an electricity pylon and turn right on a woodland path. When it forks, branch left across the wooded lower slopes of Haughmond (pronounced Hormond) Hill, and continue to meet a road opposite the entrance to Abbey Wood (Haughmond Hill, 124).

Turn left for a few strides and then go right, along the access to Haughmond Abbey (123). At the end of the drive go over a stile to the left of the abbey entrance, and follow a fence round the perimeter of the grounds, finally rising to meet a forestry trail through Abbey Wood. Cross this and go forward through a narrow belt of undergrowth to a stile over a wall.

Church Farm at More
The River Tern at Isombridge

A timber-framed cottage on Gooseberry Lane, Grinshill
St Alkmund's, Shrewsbury

Cross the ensuing pasture, half-right to meet the access drive to Haughmond Farm at its junction with the B5062, and then turn left along the driveway towards the farm.

Go past the farm buildings to continue on a long, broad farm track leading due north to a gate close by Ebury Hill, which is the site of a prehistoric fort. From the gate go left alongside a fence to a wooden kissing gate giving into a large open pasture. Go forward a short distance and then bear right, cutting across the pasture to the far corner at the junction between New Coppice and Colins Rough. In the corner you will find a stile, but do not cross it. Instead turn right, staying within the pasture and going initially along the edge of woodland, and when its boundary turns away keep on in the same direction across the pasture to a stile on the far side.

Beyond this cross a field track and go forward along the edge of the next field. The accompanying hedgerow guides you round to a stile, and from this head in the same direction across the ensuing field, aiming just to the right of Wheatley Farm. A broad track leads you towards the farm. Cross a section of rough ground to a bridge spanning a brook, and beyond this follow the continuation of the track around bends to a metal gate. Go left at the gate and walk out to the A53 at Upper Astley, near the Dog in the Lane pub.

Cross the road and go down to Astley village (121), turning left at the church. At the next bend leave the road, on the left, by turning onto a rough track. Just after a garage on the right, leave the track, going to the right of a wall to find a stile. Beyond this go forward along the left field edge, and in the ensuing meadow keep on in the same direction to a stile in the far corner. Cross the next field, going half-right, then go over a stile onto the on-going path, and cross two fields to reach the A49.

Cross the A49, a narrow field and the railway beyond, and then, in a large open pasture dotted with trees, bear slightly right aiming to the right of a red-brick farmhouse, Wood Farm, in the distance. To the right of the farmhouse a metal gate gives onto a surfaced lane. Turn right towards the village of Hadnall (121).

About 100m/yds before rejoining the A49, turn left across a field, heading for the church. At a lane turn left and 30m/yds later turn right over a stile and go forward past an electricity transformer and on to a gate near a pond. Cross a stile and head across the next field to a concealed stile in a corner, about 20m/yds to the left of a power line pole in a hedgerow. Go forward to meet a rough-surfaced lane and turn right to meet and cross a road. Walk along the edge of the next field and then along an enclosed pathway which comes out into an open field. Cross this to a stile opposite and then keep forward along a field edge to meet Mill Lane.

Go diagonally right for a few strides, and then left onto a green pathway behind a cottage built with large sandstone blocks.

Keep on through a small woodland and on across an arable field. In the next field go half-left to a stile. Cross another field to an enclosed path and into light woodland surrounding Hardwicke Stables.

The woodland path brings you out onto a lane. Turn left, and a short distance further, opposite the entrance to the stables, turn right on a field edge track. Keep going until, at the northern edge of woodland, you meet a farm track.

[From this point the right of way goes forward across a field to intersect a hedge, but there is, at the time of writing, no way through the hedge, and the field edge track is the only option.]

Turn right and follow it until you meet a lane. Go diagonally right for a few strides to a stile. In the next field, go half-right to another stile. After this, cross the next one, and then go up two fields to emerge onto a short, overgrown track leading to Sandy Lane.

Turn left and walk up to the village of Grinshill (119). At a T-junction turn right and then take the first on the left to go past All Saints' Church.

GRINSHILL TO WEM
Distance: 6.4km (4 miles)

At the top of the lane, as it bends to the right, go with it, but then immediately left behind an isolated sandstone building to gain a path ascending into woodland.

Ignore a stile on the left, but shortly afterwards, when the path forks, go left and immediately left again on a rising path. The paths are confusing, but if in doubt keep going up, the steepest way, and eventually you will join a horizontal track. Turn right to reach a sandy lane. Alternatively, if you turn left along the horizontal track you can follow it to the summit of Grinshill Hill (118); then retrace your steps.

Turn right along the lane and go past a cottage to a signposted footpath on the left. Leave the lane at this point and turn left past an isolated cottage to a stile. Go down the ensuing field, a hedgerow on your right; ignore the first gate on the right, but at the second, near a pond, go through a gate, and turn sharp left along a hedgerow to a stile at a lane on the edge of Clive (118).

Go right for 20m/yds, and then left over a stile, and along a field edge. Another stile...another field edge...take the route on in the same direction. When the fence bends to the right, leave it, and go slightly left across a field, keeping to the left of a pond to reach a stile in a hedgerow.

The stile gives onto a rough track. Cross this and the stile beyond, and keep forward along a left field margin to reach a pond, where the Way continues by stiles to a gate onto another rough lane.

Follow the lane for 200m/yds, and then leave it, left, over a stile, before going ahead along a left field margin to a stile. Cross this into a large pasture but keep forward, always following the left-hand hedgerow, for about 500m/yds to another stile. Once over this, change to the other side.

A stile at the bottom of the field then gives onto a large open pasture, with the path striking forward to the left of Trench Hall. Follow this obvious path, leading over stiles to a lane. Cross the lane beside a cottage and go forward down a green track to a stile. Over the stile, go half-left to another cottage, keeping to the right of it, to reach a lane at Tilley Green.

Cross the lane to a stile; once over this pass between two ponds and keep forward across a large open pasture, parallel with overhead power lines. Keep on to reach Pankeymoor Cottages, and there follow an access track out to the B5476. When you reach the road turn right past Oaklands and follow the road as it passes beneath the railway bridge and leads up into Wem (116).

WEM TO STANTON UPON HINE HEATH
Distance: 9.6km (6 miles)

At the top of Mill Street turn right and walk as far as the station. Over the railway line, turn right into Aston Road, and keep on until about 40m/yds after a small supermarket (and opposite Southlands), you can turn right onto a gravel track (signposted to Barker's Green). Keep forward along the ensuing field edge to a stile, and then strike across the next field to cross the River Roden at a footbridge. Follow the path to a stile and over this turn right on a surfaced lane.

At a T-junction at Barker's Green turn left for 130m/yds, and then turn right into a green lane. Follow this out to a lane, turn right and walk along the lane for 1km (half a mile). Just after Hill Cop Bank Farm, as the road bends sharply left, you can leave it for a signposted footpath that leads down steps (very slippery, especially when wet) through light woodland. When you emerge from the woodland, go forward and cross the River Roden once more.

On the other side go forward up a field, walking parallel with an overhead cable. At the top turn right and walk out to meet a lane that leads into the village of Lee Brockhurst (114). Cross the River Roden once again and then the A49, and head onto a rising green lane. Beyond its high point the lane descends through a sandstone cutting and continues to meet another lane at which you turn sharp left. Follow the on-going track to cross the River Roden for the fourth and final time at Papermill Bridge.

Beyond, keep left of a cottage to ascend a sunken green lane to Papermill House. Keep on for another 100m/yds and then leave it, on the right, over a stile, and go forward alongside a fence towards a plantation. Go down through this, and forward along a track, but soon leaving it, on the left, over a stile to go along the left edge of a large arable field.

At the far corner of the field go left through a gate and immediately over a stile, and then forward across another arable field. In the next field go diagonally across the middle and, when you reach a rough-surfaced lane, turn right.

After about 250m/yds, leave the lane at a waymarked stile on the left and enter a field, then go forward along the left-hand edge. At the far side cross a stile into an arable field. Follow the field edge around two sides, and then from a fence corner strike diagonally right on a path that leads out to a lane just north of Stanton upon Hine Heath (113). Walk down the lane, cross a road junction and go forward towards the church (signposted).

STANTON UPON HINE HEATH TO HIGH ERCALL
Distance: 11.3km (7 miles)

Just as you reach Church Road, with the church off to your right, turn left into Church Lane. At its end cross a small field and then keep to the left edge of the next to a stile in a corner. Go forward alongside a fence and then beside a small plantation before going down to walk parallel with the River Roden for a short distance. Cross a feeder stream, and then strike across the next field towards Sowbath Farm.

As you reach the farm go through a metal gate and across the farmyard beyond to a surfaced access. Follow this out to the A53. Cross this, and in the field beyond go half-right, roughly heading for the Wrekin, which looms in the distance. Make a mid-field adjustment to head towards the right-hand side of a barn-like structure, close by which there is a stile immediately adjoining an oak tree.

Cross the left-hand margin of the next field to a broad grassy track. Turn right on this and walk out to a road. At the road turn right, and follow it as far as Muckleton Hall Farm.

When you reach the farm turn right beside barns onto a concrete access leading to a broad track. Keep on along this until near its end you can leave it, on the left, to cross two fields, aiming for a stag-headed oak (i.e. a tree with bare branches protruding above its leafy canopy) in a hedgerow in the distance. From the oak strike out across arable fields, often cropped over, heading for houses ahead.

Eventually, you intercept a broad farm track and can follow this out to a road. Cross the road, going forward down a lane opposite. Just by Wytheford House Farm, as the road bends left, leave it by going right on a dirt track (Great Wytheford, 112). A short way on leave the track by going left over a stile, and then down the left-hand field boundary to another stile. From this cross the next field, keeping slightly left of an isolated sycamore tree in mid-field to locate a stile in a corner.

Cross a brook and walk out past houses to reach a road at a bridge spanning the River Roden. Turn right, and walk up to Poynton Green, there going left to Poynton. Keep on down the lane to Poynton Manor Farm and just opposite the remains of an old chapel incorporated into farm buildings go left over a stile and down the ensuing field to a footbridge at the bottom.

Climb through light woodland to a hedgerow gap, and go forward across fields to meet a concrete track. Cross the track and keep on in the same direction to a hedge corner, and then go alongside the hedge to a dirt track. Turn right and walk out to a lane.

[NOTE: From the hedgerow gap above, an alternative route has recently been waymarked. This is a 'permissive' route devised by the landowner, but it is not a right of way. Parts of it are not easy to walk, and it is longer than the correct route.]

Turn left and follow the lane to High Ercall (110).

HIGH ERCALL TO IRONBRIDGE
Distance: 26.3km (16½ miles)

At the end of Park Lane cross the village road and go forward into Church Road to pass the church of St Michael and All Angels. Just past the church turn right through a wooden gate onto an enclosed pathway that brings you out onto Shirlowe Lane. Cross this, and go through a double metal gate opposite to follow the right-hand edge around two fields.

Go past a sewage works and across a field to a stile and gate near a power line. Turn right onto a surfaced track, and after about 250m/yds turn left through gates and go forward with an established hawthorn hedgerow on your left. At the end of the hedgerow go through a gap and turn right, then walk on to meet a farm track at a stile/gate.

About 80m/yds after the turning to Sugdon Farm, turn left along a green lane that steers you out to a road at a junction. Go forward into the road opposite (signposted for Marsh Green and Isombridge). Follow the lane to a junction, and turn right to reach Isombridge Farm.

As the road bends sharply right in front of the farm, leave it, on the left, to pass around farm buildings to a gate giving onto open pasture adjoining the River Tern. Cut across to the river and follow its bank to a footbridge on the edge of Allscott (109). Over the bridge go through a garden area and walk out to a road, turn right and keep on to the Plough Inn at Cross Green junction.

Cross the road, a stile, the ensuing field and a railway line. On the other side head for an oak tree in mid-field, and then keep on in the same direction to reach and walk alongside a hedgerow. Cross a stile on the right and go around the left edge of a paddock to emerge on a lane near Tiddicross Stables.

Turn right for 60m/yds, and then go left, across a field to a stile in a hedgerow, keeping on in the same direction to meet a surfaced lane. Turn right through Leaton and go up to a road junction and turn right again. Walk up to meet the busy B5061 at Overley and turn left, walking alongside the B-road for 800m/yds until you can turn right at a junction on the road to Aston.

Cross the A5 bridge, and go on for about 40m/yds until you can descend right, down a stepped embankment. At the bottom go right, back towards the A5, and then walk along a field edge, parallel with the road, to reach a stile in a corner. Over this go half-left across an arable field to a hedge corner. Keep to the right of the hedge for a few strides, and then go through a gap to walk along the other side as far as a field track which will take you, left, to a group of farm buildings at Aston.

After emerging onto the road at Aston Farm turn right to a T-junction near Aston Hall Farm, and then turn left along a lane that leads to the road known as Wrekin Course. Walk left along Wrekin Course for 1km (half a mile) until you can leave it at a waymarked stile on the right, giving onto a path that crosses an arable field to reach the edge of the woodland that cloaks the Wrekin.

Enter the woodland and turn right on a woodland track, following this upwards until it meets another track at a U-bend near a large beech tree. Turn right and walk up to the summit of the Wrekin (106).

Once you've gained the top the downhill route is obvious,

descending steeply, except for a cruel interlude when the Way rises onto Little Hill. At the bottom of the descent, cross a stile beside a gate onto Spout Lane.

Turn left and walk along Spout Lane for 3km (2 miles) until, on the edge of Little Wenlock, you can leave it, on the right just after Holly Cottage, and go forward along the edge of two fields and across a third to a stile giving access to a brief hedgeway. At the end of this walk out along a gravel track and follow Witchwell Lane up to St Lawrence's Church (Little Wenlock, 105).

[Anyone wanting to go through Little Wenlock need only follow the road past Holly Cottage, later turning right opposite the Huntsman pub and walking down to the church.]

Turn right, and follow the road round until it branches, and here go right, down Buildwas Lane. Follow the lane, surfaced at first and then becoming stony and rough. Leave the track, on the left, at a metal gate and stile. Go forward on a grassy path between hawthorns, hazel, elder and holly to reach the edge of a large open pasture. Keep on for 40m/yds, and then go left on an ascending path to reach another field. At the top of the path turn right and head for two radio masts.

Between the masts cross a stile and go round two edges of the ensuing arable field until you can walk out onto an access track to Moors Farm.

[NOTE: Between the masts and Moors Farm access the landowner has re-routed the Way onto the line described above. This has not been done officially, and the right of way, which is often cropped, crosses the field diagonally to the farm track.]

Follow the track out to a road junction and turn right. Cross a bridge and immediately turn left towards Leasows Farm. Just as you reach the farm, go right, through a white gate, and down the next field to reach a stile giving access to Lydebrook Dingle.

Follow the path through the dingle, branching right at a path junction, and eventually you emerge onto a broad path. This takes you into a large meadow, following an old track, the Rope Walk (104), which brings you out at a road, opposite the entrance to a Quaker burial ground (103). Turn left and descend to a junction just before a railway viaduct. Turn right into Darby Road, walking alongside the viaduct (Darby family, 102). Further on you pass beneath the arches and walk past the Museum of Iron and up to the main Coalbrookdale road. Turn right (Coalbrookdale, 102).

Follow the road until you can branch left at the youth hostel, at Paradise. After 100m/yds turn left up a surfaced lane, and at the top go forward and just to the right of a metal gate onto a footpath between hedges, climbing into the woodland cover of Lincoln Hill (101).

When you reach a crosspath, turn right, descending to leave the woodland near some cottages. Go forward until you meet a surfaced lane, descending. At this point, keep left in front of more cottages, and you will come onto a woodland path (signposted to Lincoln Hill Road). Just after a stile start climbing left on a flight of steps (signposted to the Rotunda). At the top of the steps bear right for a few strides, and then turn left up more steps to reach the ruined remains of the Rotunda, from which there is an excellent view over the Ironbridge Gorge.

Keep on along a woodland path. When it forks, turn right for Lincoln Hill Road, and as you reach a driveway, turn left and walk out to a road. Turn sharp right and then take the second road on the left (Church Hill). Follow this down to a roundabout at the bottom, and turn right to walk into Ironbridge (99).

The final section can be shortcut at a few places as you descend Church Hill, notably via a flight of steps at the entrance to St Luke's Church, which passes beneath the church grounds and descends into Ironbridge at the Tontine Hotel.

SECTION 2: IRONBRIDGE TO LUDLOW

South from Ironbridge the Way continues with an energetic ascent onto Benthall Edge, and maintains this attitude for much of the distance. It's all quite splendid walking, with numerous ups and downs, and countless beautiful cameos around almost every corner. And perhaps the finest of these is kept until last – the stunning view of Ludlow from the heights of Knowbury.

Logistically, this section of the walk, notably beyond Much Wenlock, is the most problematic. Small villages – Easthope, Holdgate and Knowbury – are passed through, but offer little sustenance to walkers. Not until Ludlow is reached can supplies be replenished, without the short diversion to Cleehill village.

The closure of the Wheathill Youth Hostel in 1998 means that there is very limited accommodation between Wilderhope Manor Youth Hostel and Ludlow, facing walkers with the prospect of a 31.5km/19½ miles day.

Between Wilderhope Manor and Ludlow, the Way also tackles two high summits, the Clee Hills, and the additional effort of getting over the two hills should be allowed for, especially in less than ideal walking weather. It may be worth considering taking a bus or a taxi into Ludlow from some mid-way point, and returning the next day to finish off.

Until the accommodation infrastructure along the Shropshire Way is more fully developed, the problems of finding somewhere to stay overnight will remain.

IRONBRIDGE TO MUCH WENLOCK
Distance: 8km (5 miles)

Cross the Iron Bridge and on the far side turn right at a metal gate that gives on to the trackbed of the former Severn Valley Railway. Either move right and go down a broad, rough-surfaced track that leads past cottages and finally passes beneath an old railway bridge, then bear right to reach the foot of a flight of steps. Or go forward along the trackbed until you pass over the bridge, and a few strides on leave the trackbed to ascend the steps into delightful woodland on a terraced path that leads to a path junction.

At the junction turn left, keeping to the left of a bench, onto a rising stepped path into Benthall Edge Wood. The steps guide you up to Benthall Edge (97), still in woodland. At the top of the steps, turn right (waymarked), and follow a path through the woodland. Keep on in the same direction, ignoring deviating footpaths, until you reach a waymark on the left just where the on-going path forks. Branch left and at the next waymark bear right to leave the wood near a cottage. At the cottage turn along a wide access track, and follow this until it meets another, and then turn sharp right to a gate.

Beyond the gate the on-going track descends slightly to a distinct bend. Leave it on the apex of the bend to go onto a rising path through more woodland to a stile in a field corner. Follow the top edge of the ensuing field to another stile, and from there head for Vineyards Farm. Past the farm, walk out to meet a lane at Wyke.

Turn right and follow the lane for some distance until just after a roadside crash barrier, you can leave the lane, on the left, at a footpath signpost, onto a stony track through woodland. When this rises to an isolated farmhouse, leave the track, branching left onto a rutted vehicle track that brings you into an arable field.

The landowner has here re-routed the Way to send you around two sides of the field until, at a waymark, you leave the field edge to dive off to the right into undergrowth and through a metal gate into the adjacent field. The correct line, however, strikes into the field (often cropped over), before turning right to the field edge.

Through the hedge, turn left along the field boundary to a stile at a hedge junction. Over this go forward beside a hedgerow for about 200m/yds, and then bear half-right to go down to Bradley Farm. Go past the farm and then out to cross a road onto a farm track opposite. At its end the track branches into two fields. Go into the one on the left and forward along a field edge to a stile in a corner. Over this follow a grassy path in the next field to a footbridge spanning a brook and take an enclosed path past two houses.

Walk out along an access track to a surfaced lane which takes you past the priory (Wenlock Priory, 94) and into Much Wenlock (93). When you reach the end of Bull Ring, at a T-junction, turn left to go past the church and the Guildhall, turning right into High Street.

MUCH WENLOCK TO EASTHOPE
Distance: 8.8km (5½ miles)

Keep on to the far end of High Street, and, at a road junction, go ahead into Victoria Road (A458). After about 350m/yds branch left on the B4371 for Wenlock Edge. When you reach the Horse and Jockey pub leave the B-road, and turn right into Blakeway Hollow, initially a narrow, surfaced lane.

Keep following the lane, which deteriorates into a dirt track between hedgerows, and finally reaches the edge of Blakeway Coppice, part of the National Trust holdings along Wenlock Edge (88, 91). Branch left here through a hedge gap and turn right along a field margin to a path that runs between a quarry on the left and the boundary of the coppice.

When, opposite the main quarry buildings, the path reaches a bridleway sign, about 1.5km/1 mile from Presthope, branch right, descending through the coppice to join a broad forest trail.

Turn left and follow the trail through delightful woodland until it rises to the Wenlock Edge car park, adjoining the B4371. Go through the car park and turn right along the road, taking care in the absence of footpaths against approaching traffic, much of which is travelling at high speed. Take the next road junction on the left, about 300m/yds distant, signposted for Bourton.

Keep on downhill as far as a footpath sign on the right. Leave the road here, and walk along a broad, overgrown track to meet a rather better one a short distance further on. Keep left, and follow the track until it branches. Go to the right and a few strides further on, branch left and pass to the right of a large shed. The on-going track shortly degenerates into a field path, cutting (usually) through crops to a stand of trees surrounding a pond in mid-field.

Continue on the other side towards another group of trees at the edge of which a stile gives access to a long, thin neck of coppice woodland. On the far side you emerge onto an old hedgeway beyond which follow the on-going hedge/fence until you can walk beside an adjacent fence going up-field to a stile in the top corner.

After the stile you enter Dove Plantation, walking up its south-western edge to a stile at the top. Keep forward, following an on-going fence/hedge along the right-hand margin of an arable field, climbing gently until you locate a stile on the right. Beyond the stile, go down through a narrow strip of woodland to enter a large, open pasture.

Cross the pasture, half-left, descending to a signpost and power lines in the distance at the edge of Natal Coppice. Keep on in much the same direction, gradually moving away from the coppice and passing beneath power lines, to a stile beside a metal gate. Beyond, follow the left-hand field edge to a vehicle track leading out to the road on the outskirts of Easthope.

Turn left, and walk down towards the village (89).

EASTHOPE TO HOLDGATE
Distance: 8km (5 miles)

In Easthope take the road for Longville and Church Stretton, passing Manor Farm to go through the village, leaving on the other side along a rising lane.

Turn left on a broad, rough vehicle track (signposted) leading to an isolated house. Go past the house to a stile beside a metal gate. Over this go forward on a broad green track. This runs on to meet a gate in a fence. Ignore this, keeping to the left of the gate, and continuing beside the fence to reach Hall Farm.

As you reach the farmyard, bear left on a broad vehicle track that takes you past Lutwyche Hall (89), and on for some distance to turn right beside Pilgrim Cottage (89). After the cottage turn left on another broad track heading for the youth hostel at Wilderhope Manor (88).

As you reach the manor, pass either side of it to reach a stile beside Wilderhope Farm. Over the stile, go forward to pass the farm, and then keep forward along a track to enter a large sloping pasture. Follow the right-hand field edge until you meet a substantial footbridge over a brook.

Across this, keep forward along the course of the brook until you can cross it at a waymarked stile and footbridge. Over the brook, bear right along a fenceline, and keep going to reach the access to Lower Stanway Farm. Turn right, away from the farm, and, having re-crossed the brook, go immediately left over a stile, then pass between the brook and a fence to another stile and footbridge.

In the ensuing field bear right, and roughly follow the course of the brook for some distance below the wooded slopes of Stanway Coppice (87) to New House Farm. As you reach the farm, with Brown Clee Hill suddenly coming into view in the distance, go right over a bridge and then half-left up the next field to a stile giving on to a lane. Turn left along the lane to a junction with the B4368.

Turn right along the B-road for about 30m/yds and then leave it, on the left, over a stile, striking down-field to a bridge spanning the River Corve.

Once over the river, go up the next two fields following the field boundary to a metal gate giving access to a lane. Cross the lane and the stile beyond, and then go along a field edge to reach Trow Brook. Cross this on stepping stones, occasionally flooded. Beyond the next stile, keep right, up the edge of fields, always heading for the church of the Holy Trinity in the village of Holdgate ahead. A concrete ramp rises to a final metal gate beside the church (Holdgate, 86).

HOLDGATE TO KNOWBURY
Distance: 19.8km (12¼ miles)

From the church, turn right and go down the road to a footpath sign on the left, immediately before Holdgate Farm. Leave the road at a gate, go down beside a barn and strike down the ensuing field to a hedge corner and then onward to a step stile in the far right-hand corner of the field.

Once over this go forward along the left-hand edge of a large pasture, following the course of a delightful old green lane between hedgerows. This ends at a plank bridge spanning a brook, and another step stile. Go on into the next field, still with a hedgerow on your left, climbing gently.

As you draw level with the isolated building of Blue Hall, go through the hedgerow at a stile, and then continue as before until the on-going hedge changes direction. When it does, keep forward across a pasture to a stile to the right of a metal gate. Beyond this go forward across the next field to reach the foot of a lightly wooded slope called Mittons Rough. Cross a stile, and then climb obliquely left through bracken to reach a waymark at the top edge of the wooded slope.

Go forward along the top of the wood until you reach a metal gate at a hedge and fence junction. Turn right here alongside a hedgerow and go through another gate a short distance away, to reach a rough farm access that takes you past Earnstrey Hall Farm to meet a lane (Earnstrey, 85).

Cross the lane and go over a stile opposite, and then forward to the right-hand field corner about 100m/yds away. Continue alongside a hedgerow in the next field, and keep going to a footbridge and stile. Beyond this, turn left, heading towards the slopes of Brown Clee ahead, and walk up the field margin, beside an established hedgerow of birch, ash, oak and hawthorn, to a gate. After this, keep on beside the on-going hedgerow. A path leads you on to pass behind New Earnstrey Park Farm, to a stile. After this go left, passing closer to the farm, and soon reaching another lane. Turn right.

Go past Park View and at the next bend leave the lane, on the right, for a stile near a metal gate, which gives onto the top of a sunken lane. Go down this to a footbridge, and then climb on the other side above the continuation of the sunken lane. This curves round, left, at the top of the field, and runs on beside a hedge to a stile in a field corner. Beyond this, turn right on a surfaced lane.

Keep along the lane for 200m/yds to a T-junction, and turn left on the lane for Ditton Priors. Keep on for about 300m/yds, and then turn right, near a telephone box, on the lane for Cockshutford. About 180m/yds up the lane, just after Bank House, turn left onto a broad, rough-surfaced track, through a gate. The track climbs eventually to pass through a gate, with improving views, and then rises to another gate, beyond which it breaks out onto the top of the bracken-covered common, Abdon Liberty, just as Clee Burf and Titterstone Clee come into view.

Through the top gate bear left, curving along the outside edge of an area of gorse that partly fills the on-going line of the old track, to rise to a stile near the top corner of a hill pasture. Over this, go half-right for a few strides and then turn right to head for Clee Burf, Brown Clee Hill's southern summit, crowned by twin navigational masts (Brown Clee Hill, 82).

[From this point walkers wanting to visit the summit of Brown Clee Hill, known as Abdon Burf, should simply follow a boggy path heading directly for the bemasted summit, and return the same way. Additional distance: 1km/half a mile.]

Continue on a broad grassy path between a fence and a spread of heather. When the fence changes direction, leave it and keep forward, still on a broad grassy track, but gradually move away from the track through bracken to head for a 'jump' stile a short distance to the left of a metal gate – most walkers, however, use the metal gate.

Beyond, go forward on a grassy path, gradually veering left to the edge of woodland, marked by a fence and wall. Soon, the fence and wall come together and the on-going path ascends beside them. Keep following the wall/fence to the south summit.

The path ends at a gate beside the relay station. Go through the gate, and move slightly right on a grassy path towards the fenced edge of an old quarry. From a fence corner, branch left on a descending path across rough, upland pasture. On the other side the path reaches the edge of woodland.

Go forward with the woodland on your left, just entering its upper edges, and eventually reaching a gate at the top of a sunken trackway. Go down here below banks of gorse and hawthorn.

After the next gate, bear right, and keep descending to reach a farm, and turn left just after the farm onto a narrow grassy path (signposted). Continue down the path, flanked by overgrown hedgerows and scrub to reach a lane near a telephone box. Cross the lane, slightly right, and then continue down a broad track, initially grassy, and then becoming rough-surfaced on reaching Newton Cottage. Beyond, it continues to Newton Farm, bearing left and descending to cross Newton Dingle, then rising steadily beyond on a long, broad track to reach the B4364 at Dodshill.

On reaching the B4364, turn right and a few strides later go left along a rough-surfaced access leading to Dodshill Farm. As you reach the first outbuildings leave the access, over a stile on the right (waymarked), and go down the next field to the bottom corner, to a stile beside a gate. Beyond this, go up beside a hedgerow towards The Knapp Farm. When you reach the farm access, turn left and walk out to a lane. Turn right, and ascend over the high point of the lane, then go down to reach Upper Bromdon Farm. Just after passing the farm, leave the lane by turning right onto an old track (Callow Lane).

At the end of Callow Lane, just before Callowgate Farm, go through a gate, and then forward along a green track through bracken, heading for the steep northern slopes of Titterstone Clee Hill. Go up the track, and when it forks branch left and climb onto the hill slopes. As you reach the edge of the summit plateau bear right, with two flat-topped radar dishes on your left, to reach the summit trig pillar (Titterstone Clee Hill, 80).

From the trig pillar head to the right of the flat-topped radar dishes to meet a service road. Leave the road, veering slightly right towards the top edge of a disused quarry, on a broad green track that later descends a ridge between two adjoining quarries (79) to reach the top of a rough stony track. Turn right and descend on this to rejoin the service road at a hairpin bend.

Go forward and cross the road twice, keeping on in the same direction to pass between the dismantled abutments of an old quarry tramway, still descending on a stony track that curves right to discover the grey ruins of the quarry buildings. Go forward through these, and bear left to the top of the Bitterley Incline. Go down the Incline as far as a concrete slab bridge, and here drop left, beside the tunnel, onto a broad green track through bracken, and then beside a hedgerow and fence.

Keep forward across a rough-surfaced lane to go down through bracken to a footbridge spanning Benson's Brook. Cross the footbridge and climb on the other side to a gate, and, beyond this, go forward with a fence and hedge on your left towards Nine Springs Farm.

Just as you reach the farm, turn right, ignoring the tempting stile and gate, and go down-field beside a post and wire fence, backed by a substantial hedgerow, to a stile.

In the next field, strike up to the left, roughly following the direction of overhead power lines, but moving away a little through bracken and gorse on an indistinct path, to reach the top far corner of the field, there crossing a fence at a fence junction. Then continue forward across the top of the next field, beside a fence and above gorse bushes, though many of these will require evasive action. By following the fence you arrive at a dark-blue metal gate in a corner.

Beyond the gate, keep on in the same direction, heading for a fence/stile, and then advance towards a clutch of sheep pens adjoining Shop Farm. On reaching the farm, and having passed through the pens, go forward through a metal gate into a large pasture, and strike half-left to another metal gate on the far side. Through this gate go along a broad green track to meet a gravel vehicle track near a modern house, and go down the track to meet Dhustone Lane at a bend. Turn right, and follow the lane to meet the A4117.

[You can detour, left, to Cleehill for supplies from this point if you need to.]

Cross the A-road and go down the broad track opposite towards farm buildings. Keep to the right of the farm and cross a stile adjoining a small barn. Walk across the next field to a fence corner, on the right, and then continue with a fence on your right to a stile and a green lane beyond.

A short way on, at a cross-track, keep forward for 40m/yds to a stile on the left (signpost). Beyond this go forward for a short distance below a post and rail fence, and then descend right to cross a brook and stile and enter a small dingle, rising in a few strides to another stile.

Go forward beside a holly hedgerow, and through a hedge gap, still maintaining the same direction to cross the top of a small field to reach an old trackway. Cross this and three small fields to a large sloping pasture. Bear right on a narrow path, and follow this, roughly contouring and then descending to a stile at a lane.

Climb immediately (without crossing the stile) to rejoin the path above, which has ignored this legality and simply used common sense to round the sloping hill and so bring you to a step stile at the rear corner of Knowbury churchyard. Go forward on a fenced grassy path to reach a surfaced area beside the church, and a lane (Knowbury, 74).

KNOWBURY TO LUDLOW
Distance: 7.2km (4½ miles)

Cross the lane at Knowbury Church and go down a signposted footpath opposite. Keep forward with a hedgerow on your left, through a hedge gap, and continue in the same direction through another gate. Then go on to reach a stile at the top of a holly-hedged lane – the stile is concealed in the left-hand corner of the field, at the junction of two hedgerows.

When you reach a lane turn right. After about 100m/yds, leave the lane at a stile on the left, and head down the next field to another stile, with a grand view of Ludlow and Mortimer Forest (67) directly ahead.

In the next field follow the hedgerow on the left for a while until it makes a pronounced turn to the left, and here leave it, going across the field in roughly the same direction, and heading for a gate, just to the right of which is a stile.

Cross the stile, and follow the left field margin ahead, then at the bottom of the field turn right along a hedge. Soon go left through a gap and forward on a broad green track across an arable field.

At the far side of the field turn right onto another track, and descend gradually to meet a prominent farm access. On reaching it, go forward through a hedge gap, and then, after about 100m/yds, at a gate/stile, turn obliquely left across a field aiming for the right-hand of two trees set in distant mid-field. As you move forward so a gate and stile come into view. Head for these.

As you enter the next field Cay Brook comes into view on your right. Go forward, bearing slightly right to parallel the brook until you can cross it at a stone bridge. Over the bridge, walk up to a stile next to a gate, and beyond follow the field boundary. A ditch accompanies the field edge and after 150m/yds cross this at a point where it is culverted and walk forward with a low hedgerow on your left. When this ends turn left and follow a more substantial hedgerow, now on your right.

The track leads on into the northern edge of Ledwyche Covert (Caynham Camp, 74). Passage through the covert is brief, and soon vehicle tracks continue forward along the base of a sloping field.

Just after the track reaches Ledwyche Pool, it meets another track at a bend. Here go forward to meet Squirrel Lane, near a large barn development, and at the lane turn left to cross Ledwyche Bridge.

About 200m/yds after the bridge, leave the lane at a bend and clamber over a double stile into a field on the right. Keep forward along the left field boundary to another stile, and then keep on in the same direction until you reach a stile and steps leading up to the Ludlow bypass. Cross this with great care and go down to a stile on the other side. Over the stile turn left and walk towards industrial units. On reaching a chain-link fence turn right to walk along a fenced pathway to Coder Road. At the road go forward to Parys Road, and turn right.

Go across the end of Blashfield Road, and 20m/yds further on turn left up a surfaced pathway into a modern housing estate. Stay on the path as it passes between houses and crosses two estate roads before reaching Dark Lane at the top side of the estate. Turn left, and at a footpath sign leave the lane, turning right and going down a grassy slope, walking directly towards St Laurence's Church in Ludlow, to enter another housing estate below.

A hedged path funnels you into the estate. Go forward to a T-junction and turn right and then take the first bend on the left (about 20m/yds further on). Follow the road as it curves to the right, but leave it for a pathway (ignore a flight of steps) on the left going down between houses to reach a railway underpass.

Through the underpass turn right along Sheet Road, left into Weeping Cross Lane, and follow this round into Temeside. At a T-junction, on a bend, go left with the River Teme on your left, to reach Ludford Bridge. [NOTE: The youth hostel is just across the bridge. At the time of writing it is up for sale. If you intend to use it, be sure to ring first.] (Ludlow, 68)

[Walkers staying in the centre of town need not go down to the Teme, but, having passed Weeping Cross Lane junction, should simply keep forward at all times to reach the Butter Cross in the centre of Ludlow, from where the on-going route continues.]

SECTION 1: LUDLOW TO SHREWSBURY

From Ludlow to the conclusion in Shrewsbury, the Way saves some of its best for last. The walk as far as Stanton Lacy is delightfully easy, as is the continuation to Onibury and Stokesay Castle. After that comes a fine romp over the hills to Clun and up to Bishop's Castle, Linley Hill and Stiperstones before descending to Bridges.

For many the final day will begin through the spellbinding landscape around Ratlinghope from where you go on to enjoy the views from Lyth Hill before finally slipping down gently to the outskirts of Shrewsbury, and the last lap.

LUDLOW TO STOKESAY CASTLE (Craven Arms)
Distance: 14.2km (9 miles)

Between Ludlow and Stokesay Castle the Way passes through Stanton Lacy and Onibury. Both are small, attractive villages, and the latter possesses a café (at the railway), a village shop and overnight accommodation, if needed.

To resume from Ludford Bridge, go forward up Lower Broad Street, through Broadgate, and into Broad Street. At the top, directly ahead, stands the Butter Cross.

At the rear of the Butter Cross, locate College Street, and turn into this to pass Hosyers Almshouses and the church of St Laurence. At a T-junction turn left to go down a narrow street, and after the last house on the right, turn right down steps to a descending walkway that leads to a road. Follow the road forward until it bends to the right. Here leave it, on the left, for a roughly surfaced lane, and after about 40m/yds, go right, through a gate into a walled pathway leading to Burway Bridge, spanning the River Corve.

Cross the bridge and go ahead to another, this time spanning a dry ditch. Through the gate beyond bear half-right across a field on a grassy path to reach Coronation Avenue near a bus stop. Turn left, and shortly left again into Burway Lane.

Follow Burway Lane, which later degenerates into a rough track.

When the road meets a surfaced lane, cross it and press on to Burway Farm. Pass the farm and keep ahead across a broad grassy strip of land to a gate. Beyond the gate follow the left field margin, which later bends right and rises to meet the A49. Ignore the bridleway on the left.

Cross the A49 with care, go forward along a B-road opposite, and over a railway bridge. When this meets the edge of Ludlow Race Course, turn right on a broad track that skirts the edge of the course (Mortimer Forest, 67; golf course, 66).

Keep on past two pairs of cottages until, about 80m/yds before a surfaced lane across the race course, you can leave the track, on the right, into trees. Look for a footpath signpost, pointing out a gate and stile on the edge of this small woodland.

Cross the stile and keep forward for a few strides and then bear slightly left to cross a ditch near the twin poles of overhead power lines. From the poles head half-left towards two isolated bushes in mid-field. As you draw level with them, so you meet the field margin beside the River Corve. Follow the river upstream to a footbridge.

Cross the bridge and go left along a field boundary to a stile. Cross this too, and press on along the ensuing field edge to a stile giving on to a broad track on the edge of Stanton Lacy. Walk forward to enter the village. At a T-junction turn left beside the church (Stanton Lacy, 65).

From Stanton Lacy, cross the bridge over the River Corve, and follow the road out to a T-junction.

[The correct line follows the course of a footpath parallel with the road, but at the time of writing this is overgrown and impassable.]

At the junction turn right and follow the road (taking care against approaching traffic) until you can leave it, after the second of two cottages, turning left on a signposted track between hedgerows.

When one of the hedgerows ends, keep on in the same direction along the edges of two fields to a couple of metal gates. Beyond these, follow the left field edge up to reach a farm access. Cross this by stiles, and go across the ensuing field, in the same direction. When you reach another lane, cross it, too, by stiles, and keep on across the next field aiming for the right-hand edge of a coppice.

On reaching the corner of the coppice, bear right across the field to an oak tree at the corner of a hedgerow, and just beyond this, cross a stile.

In the next field, go left and down towards a large old oak tree, and another stile beyond. Then head across to a hedge corner, and go forward along a tall hedgerow to a stile, and then down, slightly left, to cross a brook by a bridge. Go up the ensuing two fields beside a hedgerow, before bearing right to reach a lane on the edge of the hamlet of Walton.

Turn left along the lane and after 300m/yds, leave it on the right, at the second of two adjacent signposted footpaths, through a metal kissing gate. Go forward along a field boundary to another gate, and in the next field head slightly left to the far corner, and the top of a farm lane.

Go down the lane to meet the road into Onibury (63). Turn right, and go past the church of St Michael, following the road round to meet the A49 and a railway crossing. Cross the tracks and then the River Onny, leaving the A49 at the first turning on the right.

Follow the road a short distance to a crossroads, near the lodge to Stokesay Court (63). Turn right (signposted: Aldon), and follow the on-going lane past Stepaside Farm until you can leave the lane, on the right (waymarked), over a stile beside a metal gate. In the ensuing field follow the right-hand hedgerow towards Stokewood Cottage, and join an enclosed pathway past the cottage.

When you reach a large open pasture, go forward up the left field edge to meet the access to Stokewood Farm. Cross this to the pasture on the other side and go right, alongside a hedge, to pass the farm. Keep on in the same direction across fields until you can branch right into the top edge of Stoke Wood.

Go down through the woodland, beside a fence, until, at the bottom, you can leave it at a stile. Having entered a large open pasture adjoining the railway line, bear left and cross fields (by stiles) to reach a couple of old limekilns, near a disused quarry (Norton Camp, 63).

After the kilns, the on-going path is a green track across fields that leads down to a metal gate and stile. Go on beside the railway to reach an access lane. Turn right and go down to a cottage near a railway crossing. Cross with care, and go down the lane on the other side and walk on, past a farm, to reach Stokesay Castle (61).

[Walkers wanting to stay overnight in Craven Arms (60) should walk on from Stokesay Castle to the main road and turn left, keeping ahead at a roundabout junction to enter the town.

To rejoin the Way the next day either retrace your steps, or, at the roundabout junction turn right on the Clun road (B4368) for about 800m/yds and then turn right at a road junction, at which the continuing route is rejoined at point 'A' below.]

STOKESAY TO CLUN
Distance: 17.8km (11 miles)

Although the Way between Stokesay Castle and Clun passes through two small villages – Kempton and Hopesay – neither provides refreshments, and walkers should ensure they are adequately equipped in that department before setting off.

At the rear of the castle go through a metal gate and forward between a hawthorn hedgerow and pond to pass beneath a railway bridge. On the other side of the railway turn right and follow an established hedgerow on the right across two fields, finally to enter the mixed woodland of Sallow Coppice (60) at a concealed stile in a field corner.

Go forward through the woodland on a clear path, leaving it after about 100m/yds over a stile on the right into the top corner of a field. Go forward down the right-hand field edge, and at the bottom turn left alongside the railway to a stile giving access to a lane. Turn right, under the railway bridge, and walk up to a road junction. Cross the junction, going forward into a lane opposite (A) (Watling Street, 59).

About 200m/yds along the lane leave it, on the left, at a stile beside a metal gate. Over the stile go ahead with a fence and then a hedgerow on your left across two fields. About 200m/yds into the third field, go left through a hedge gap, and, with a hedgerow now on your right, go forward, heading for a waymarked stile on the far side of the field.

Cross a lane and go over two stiles into the next field, heading up-field alongside a hedgerow on your right. Then, as you pass two oak trees in mid-field, start to move away from the hedge slightly, heading for a kissing gate on the far side of the field.

Cross a farm access (Sibdon Carwood, 58) and go across the end of a small pasture beyond to a bridge and stile giving onto a large open field. Go forward, bearing slightly right, aiming for a cottage partly concealed in the trees ahead. Cross a stile to the left of the cottage and then up the ensuing field following a hedgerow on the right.

The hedgerow guides you up to the edge of woodland, where a boundary fence leads you on to a gate and a rising track.

Go up the track with a fence on your left and then keep forward along the top edge of woodland until you encounter a ruined brick building. Go left here and pass it, and then go up to a gate. Beyond the gate keep on in the same direction, still with woodland on your left, and now rising gently onto the top of Hopesay Hill (58).

When you reach a gate at the top corner of the woodland, go forward in the same direction, targeting a farm on the far side of the valley below. Then go down on a grassy path through bracken (without losing too much height initially), and when the village of Hopesay comes into view, bear left towards it.

The path brings you down to a large oak tree at the top of a brief hedged lane. Go down the lane, passing through a gate, and on past a cottage. Follow the lane to a junction and turn left. 250m/yds further on turn left again into Hopesay (57).

Just after passing the telephone box, turn right and go up to pass St Mary's Church. Continue past the church, and at the rear of it, when the track forks, branch right on a rising track between hedgerows. When the track enters a sloping pasture, go up to its top right-hand corner, aiming for a small stand of oak trees. When you reach the trees continue climbing, keeping on in the same direction across an open pasture.

As you reach a track junction at a trio of gates, choose the third gate, and press on alongside a hedgerow on the left, rising gently to reach a gate near the high point on the track. The gate gives onto a wide open pasture. Go half-right across the pasture to a gate giving onto a farm access. Turn left and follow the descending track to Kempton (56).

On reaching the road, turn right for 100m/yds, and just after Old Kempton Stores, now only a white-painted cottage, turn left down a concrete track. At the second metal gate on the right, leave the track, cross a narrow enclosure, and then follow a grassy path across a meadow, giving onto another access track. Turn left along the track to a gate, and go forward across a gravel track between cottages to a white gate.

Beyond the gate go towards and then follow the left-hand field boundary which guides you to a stile by which you access a small enclosure, leaving by another stile a few strides away, to turn right onto another farm access. A few paces further on, branch left and keep on along the track to Lodge Farm. As you approach the farm, keep ahead in the same direction to pass it on a rising track.

About 100m/yds after the farm leave the track, branching left onto a grassy track that goes past a row of old cottages and then continues as a path into mixed woodland, running roughly parallel with a brook on your left. The path finally rises to meet a broad farm track. Turn left and pass through a gate, then keep going to Stanley Cottage.

Use a stile to gain a path going in front of the cottage, and then follow a rising access track out to meet a surfaced lane. Turn right, ascending for about 200m/yds, and then turn left into the Forestry Commission site of Bury Ditches hill-fort (55).

[The original line of the Shropshire Way does not turn left, but continues downhill to a gate and footpath on the left. Through the gate go forward to the edge of the Forestry Commission plantation, and, continuing always in the same direction, climb steadily to a high point where the Bury Ditches alternative rejoins – point 'B' below.]

Having left the road, go up a rising path to the top of Sunnyhill, which is occupied by the Iron Age hill-fort of Bury Ditches. Cross a stile beside a gate and go forward through the ramparts of the fort on a green track, with an optional diversion to a viewpoint that embraces, among others, the Clee Hills, Long Mynd, Stiperstones, Radnor Forest and the Black Mountains.

Return to the main track through the hill-fort and turn right, following this down to a stile beside a gate. Over the stile, turn right and follow a forest trail out to a T-junction (B). Turn left and descend on a track. When it joins another track, keep forward. Just after the on-going track starts to descend again, leave it on the left, at a bend, onto a signposted track shared by the Jack Mytton Way, Wild Edric's Way and the Shropshire Way.

Keep on down a hedged lane, which eventually descends to an

isolated cottage, and here turns right onto a surfaced lane. A short way on, when the lane forks, branch left to go down between the buildings of Guilden Down Farm, keeping left just after the farm on a descending lane.

Continue for 1km (over half a mile) to a waymarked stile on the right, and then curve across the ensuing field on a green track, through a hedge gap, and on to another stile. Cross a final field before Clun is reached, following a field path down to Mill Barn cottage, which you pass on an enclosed path. Then go down an access track to meet the lane left earlier. Walk along this to pass Clun Youth Hostel. Keep following the lane as it bends left and then right, and climbs gently up Newport Street, before descending to the Enfield Street-Castle Street junction (Clun, 52).

Cross the road here and go forward on a surfaced track leading to the entrance to Clun Castle.

CLUN TO BISHOP'S CASTLE
Distance: 17.5km (11 miles)

From Clun to Bishop's Castle there is no scope for taking refreshments along the way, so be sure to go adequately supplied.

At the top of the track leading into the grounds of Clun Castle turn right over a stile beside a gate and go down a grassy path and around a field edge. Shortly, move right at a gate into the adjoining field, and then go a few strides further before crossing another stile onto a roughly surfaced lane.

Turn left and go past some cottages onto a broad green track that runs beside the River Unk, which it shortly crosses by a footbridge. Beyond, it follows a field boundary, still beside the river. After another footbridge keep right alongside a small woodland boundary until you can cross an adjoining fence at a stile, and then go left to follow an old green lane.

The lane eventually runs out to meet a road. Cross it, slightly right, and go over another stile. Go forward around the left field margin to a stile in a corner, and then go left beside a hedge to begin the steady climb onto Cefns ridge.

At a footpath sign at the top of the first rise bear right, away from the fence. The path leads up to another stile, beyond which the Way continues its ascent of the ridge. When you reach a gate and stile, go slightly left, ignoring a gate on the left to follow instead a rising green lane.

The way onwards up Cefns is never in doubt, and rises steadily to the highest point of the ridge. Just beyond this, at a stile, go half-left down-field to the far left corner. Cross a stile and follow an obvious on-going track to a metal gate, and then along another hedged green lane that takes you down to a surfaced lane at Three Gates Farm.

Go forward past the farm buildings, and past two junctions, left and right, then 50m/yds later leave the road just before a house on the right, walking up to a stile, beyond which you ascend another hedged green lane. Keep climbing beside a fence, on a path that continues to rise across the eastern slopes of Hergan, and at a ridge fence, over a stile, bear half-left, initially aiming for a white farm building in the distance.

The descending track brings you down almost to reach a surfaced lane, but about 40m/yds before reaching it, branch sharp right onto the Offa's Dyke Path, which here descends parallel with a fence to a waymark. At the waymark turn left, to continue on an obvious path alongside a fence, eventually descending to cross a brook by a footbridge. On the other side, cross a stile and climb once more along Offa's Dyke Path into Eaton's Coppice. Go past the Corvedale Care Centre at Middle Knuck. Cross the access and go down the right-hand edge of the field opposite.

Descend to cross another brook, and begin climbing to cross one last ridge, at the top of which you meet a surfaced lane. Bear right for a few strides, and then leave the lane, over a stile and go down a sunken trackway, descending into Churchtown Wood. A steeply descending path leads to the bottom edge of the wood (Churchtown, 49; Offa's Dyke, 49). Don't cross the stile that faces you, but ascend, right, to another, a little higher, that gives access to a path running along the bottom edge of Churchtown Wood.

The path runs on to meet a surfaced lane at a gate and stile. Go left down the lane. At a T-junction turn right, and 20m/yds later, leave the lane on the right, over a stile at a signposted footpath. In the ensuing field, go left, rising to cross two stiles into a plantation. A few strides beyond the second stile you reach a forest track.

Turn left, and walk out to meet a surfaced lane. Turn left, immediately crossing the River Unk, and walk up to a T-junction.

At the T-junction go forward over a stile between two metal gates, and follow a rising holloway. Turn left at the top, through a gate onto a stony track heading up-field. A few strides on the track forks. Branch left onto a green track that climbs to the top left-hand corner of the field, and turn right there alongside a hedge to a metal gate. Just here you rejoin the stony track left earlier.

Beyond the gate go forward on a gradually rising track. Keep going, following the track as it bends slightly and passes between rows of hawthorns eventually to reach a lane. Turn left along the lane, and after 40m/yds leave it, on the right, to go past some farm buildings and forward along the left-hand edge of the field beyond. Follow this round to cross a stile. After the stile turn right, and a few strides later cross a post and wire fence and turn left. Go down beside the fence.

At the bottom of the field, turn right and walk down a holloway, crossing a fence on the way, to Middle Woodbatch Farm.

Go past the farm, and out along its access lane. Continue down the lane, and follow it when it bends left. Shortly after crossing a brook leave the lane, on the right, at a metal gate. Beyond the gate go forward across the bottom edge of several fields, walking roughly parallel with the brook.

Keep on until, just after a small disused quarry, you can bear left uphill to a fence/hedge corner. Go forward alongside the fence to a stile, and then keep on in the same direction across two fields.

At the far side of the second field you meet a rough vehicle track. Go forward over a stile, and continue to a stile beside a gate, then keep following the track until, just after another gate, it bends left. Here leave the track and go forward instead along a green hedgeway that leads to a gate/stile near Field Cottage, at the top of Field Lane.

Go forward down the lane and at the bottom turn right to meet Church Street. Turn left and walk to a T-junction. Turn right and then left at the Six Bells pub to walk up the main street of Bishop's Castle (44).

BISHOP'S CASTLE TO BRIDGES
Distance: 18.5km (11½ miles)

Between Bishop's Castle and Bridges the only opportunity to obtain refreshments is at Lydham, where there is an excellent and well-stocked wholefood shop and tourist information point. The shop is open Monday-Saturday, 0900-1730.

Walk up the High Street and at the top go forward into Bull Street, at the end of which turn left to Castle Green. As soon as you reach it, leave the road, on the left, passing between houses to a stile near garages. Over the stile bear half-right down the ensuing field to a stile in the bottom corner. Follow a green path half-left across the next field, which leads to another stile, concealed in a hawthorn hedgerow. Beyond this go slightly right to a stile sheltering below a sycamore tree. In the ensuing field roughly follow the right-hand hedge to another corner stile, after which the on-going path descends towards the edge of a plantation ahead, and continues down beside it to a road.

Ahead are the grassy summits of Heath Mynd, Cefn Gunthly and Corndon Hill, which sit either side of the Anglo-Welsh border. The path descends to a road junction at which you reach one of the closest points of the Way to the Welsh border.

At the road junction turn right on the B4385, but leave it after 200m/yds at a signposted footpath on the left near Upper Heblands Farm. Head diagonally across the field to the far corner, go through a gap, and bear left, roughly following a fence/hedge on the left, and keep tracking it around until you can pass into the adjoining pasture at a gate and stile. In the next field bear right on a path moving away from the fenceline, and running down to a stile in the bottom corner.

Beyond the gate, bear right along a vehicle track that runs on to meet the A488. Here turn left towards Lydham (43). Go past a road junction, and immediately leave the main road opposite Rose Cottage at a signposted footpath. A few strides on, cross a stile on the left, and go half-right across the ensuing field to the far corner. Cross the next field towards an isolated oak tree, keeping on beyond that to the far left field corner and there cross a footbridge and a stile.

Follow a green path across the next field, and when it forks branch left to the northern edge of More and a lane. Cross a stile and go through a small metal gate opposite (More, 42).

[There is an optional diversion here into the village, which can be effected by branching right instead of left when the green path forks.]

From the small gate strike across the ensuing field, aiming for the left-hand one of two tall trees on the skyline ahead. Cross two stiles in quick succession and go on across another field to a lane. Turn left and walk to a T-junction. Turn right, passing Linley Hall (41). Keep on to cross the River West Onny and take the next road on the left (signposted to The Bog).

When you reach the southern edge of Hayes Wood leave the ascending surfaced lane and branch right onto a stony track. When this forks, branch left to a gate at the top edge of the wood, and then continue rising on a broad green track flanked by beech trees (41).

When you finally break free of the avenue of trees keep forward to a stile beside a gate in a fence. Then keep on across the flank of Linley Hill (the highest point of which is known as Norbury Hill) to a metal gate from where there is a fine view northwards to Stiperstones and west into the border hills of Wales.

From the gate keep on in the same direction, following a further line of ancient beech trees and the course of a sunken way, finally curving left on a green path to a stile/gate. Beyond this, go left beside a fence and later alongside the edge of a plantation to enter the next pasture. Head for a solitary ash tree, and then go steeply down to a road.

Turn right and pass Ridge Farm, following the road round until you can leave it at a stile on the left. Descend right, into light woodland, to a stile and footbridge, and then go straight up the next field, aiming to the right of a cottage, where another stile puts you on a rough-surfaced lane. Go right for a few strides, and then leave the lane, ascending left and climbing steeply into the large plantation that cloaks the southernmost end of Stiperstones ridge.

At the highest point of the rising track, leave it, on the right, for a waymarked path that passes close by a large outcrop where, it is thought, there used to be a house, Rock House.

The path is occasionally sketchy, but never strays far from the plantation edge, and later crosses a cleared area before entering the cover of the trees once more. Cross a broad forest track and keep forward into more tree cover. When this ends at a large open pasture, go forward along the course of an old hedgerow of which only a solitary hawthorn and isolated rowans and birches remain. Cross a lane and go forward over stiles onto the southern end of the main Stiperstones ridge, here entering Stiperstones National Nature Reserve.

Follow a rising path through gorse, and when this forks, branch left, heading for Cranberry Rock, and so begin the traverse of Stiperstones ridge (36-38). Keep just to the left of Cranberry Rock, and a path, sketchy at first, will bring you out to join a more pronounced stony track along the ridge. The track goes past Manstone Rock, the highest point of the ridge, and, a short way on, past another outcrop, known as the Devil's Chair.

The track starts to descend slightly and eventually reaches a junction. There are two possibilities here: one branches right and descends to the boundary of the nature reserve at a stile and gate; the other continues further along the main track, almost to Shepherd's Rock, there doubling back, right, to go down to the stile and gate.

Over the stile, keep forward on a descending grassy track. From the next gate bear half-right down a field to a well-used farm track, and follow this past The Hollies Farm down to a T-junction. Turn right and walk down a surfaced lane to another T-junction at Bridges (34; Long Mynd, 34). Turn left, and shortly turn right to pass the Horseshoe Inn and the youth hostel.

BRIDGES TO SHREWSBURY
Distance: 25.75km (16 miles)

Walk along the road beyond the youth hostel until you can leave it, on the left, over a stile, just before a bridge. Go forward on a green path, and when you reach a single-arch bridge, bear left to another stile and turn right to enter a plantation. When you emerge from the plantation cross a track (which leads, right, to Ratlinghope, 33), and keep on to go around the edge of a large garden. The path follows a brook to a bridge and ford, and here bears left, climbing a little onto the higher of two paths. When this forks, keep forward (right-hand branch) and descend to cross a brook. Keep on in the same direction.

The path guides you towards Lower Darnford Farm, but just as you approach the farm cross a stile and then turn left, rising on a stony track. When this forks, branch right to a stile, and then bear right along the course of an old hedgerow to a signpost. Turn left on a path ascending onto a small knoll and go forward along the crest of this, then continue on a grassy path through bracken to a stile. Beyond, follow a path into the Golden Valley.

Follow the course of the main valley, climbing to meet a fence beyond which you join the Portway (33). Turn left and follow this out to meet a lane. Cross into the field beyond, heading for a solitary boundary stone, and from the stone strike north-east to two stiles close by the top of Wilderley Hill. Over these bear half-left to a slight mound, aiming for the left edge of a stand of conifers. You cross the high point of the ridge ahead through a low gap about 60m/yds away from the edge of the plantation, then keep forward, descending on a green track.

The track leads you down to a stile/gate, and from here go forward, descending to a gate at the bottom of the field. From the gate, go half-right towards the left-hand edge of a small woodland. In the bottom right-hand corner of the field, cross a stile, a farm track and another stile to enter the field opposite. Go down-field to the bottom right-hand corner, and keep on into a broad green lane.

When you reach a road at Wilderley Hall Farm (Wilderley, 32), turn right down a lane, following this for a little over 2km (1 mile) until, just before Cottage Farm, you can leave the lane, on the left, over a stile, and cross a field to a stile and footbridge on the other side. In the ensuing field, turn right around the field boundary to enter and cross a meadow, keeping on in the same direction to another footbridge. Follow a post and wire fence across the next field to a lane.

Cross the lane, slightly right, leaving it a few strides later over a stile. Go forward along the left-hand edge of two fields, linked by a footbridge, to another lane. The next field is an arable field, and in this go forward a little with the left-hand field boundary before starting to move away, slightly right, aiming for the left-hand edge of a small stand of trees on the skyline ahead.

When you reach a farm track cross it and go forward along the course of an old green lane, staying with the path when, for a short distance, it slips out of the tree cover to go along the edge of a field. The old green lane brings you down to a ford and footbridge. Continue on the track beyond, which takes you up to Vinnals Farm.

Go left through the farmyard and onward down a lane. At a T-junction turn right and walk down a lane until, after the last house on the left, you can leave the lane over a stile, and go a short distance into the next field and left over another stile. Turn right to walk parallel with a hedgerow on your right, up the ensuing field.

At the top of the field cross a couple of stiles near an old chapel, and gain the track that runs away from it. Follow this to a junction and then bear left. Go down to meet a road, and turn left for about 100m/yds, and then leave the road, on the right, along a broad stony track. When the track swings sharply to the left, leave it by going forward onto a rising track to a metal gate and beyond on to Lyth Hill (30).

Ascend onto the hill with improving views eastward, and keep on to pass a toposcope at the highest point, continuing beyond that down a stony lane (though there is a parallel green path in adjacent open hill pasture). The track brings you down to meet a lane at a rough parking area.

From the car park (on Lyth Hill) walk out along the lane until, just at a reservoir compound, you can leave the track, on the left, at a signposted footpath. Cross an arable field, and keep forward following a post and wire fence towards Lythwood Farm. Pass through the farmyard and walk out along its access to the edge of the Bayston Hill housing estate. Go across a road junction into Lythwood Road.

[NOTE: As you walk out from Lythwood Farm, the route of the Shropshire Way appears to dive into a hedgerow, just opposite an isolated house. Through the hedge it crosses a stile and turns right down an enclosed pathway, continuing past allotments and garages to meet Lythwood Road about 130m/yds from the road junction. This is the right of way; the farm access between the house and the junction is not, though it is evidently well used by locals.]

Go down Lythwood Road, passing some shops, and then turn left into Castle Lane (Bayston Hill, 29). When the lane bends right, go forward beside a house and over a stile, turning left to walk around the edge of an arable field. At the bottom left corner of a field, go forward through a narrow strip of enclosed land, and beyond that keep on along a hedgerow to a gate. Through the gate go forward to meet a lane.

Turn right, and when the lane bends right a short way on, leave it, on the bend, at a stile. In the next field, turn left to another stile/gate.

Turn right on a main road, cross the A5, and descend to a low point in the road, and there leave it, over a stile on the left. Follow the edge of the ensuing field, but only as far as a stile on the right. Cross this, and go left into a thin strip of woodland above a brook. Cross the brook and go up a footpath alongside an iron railing fence, keeping forward behind houses to a footbridge across Rea Brook (Rea Brook Valley, 28).

Go on across another footbridge and up to meet a road. Turn right, and go past Meole Brace School and on as far as the entrance to Holy Trinity Church (Meole Brace, 28). Follow the road to the left to meet Vicarage Road. Go down the road, and just as you reach the old school turn left into Meole Walk, and after 40m/yds branch right on a path at the rear of gardens.

The path brings you to a railway line. On the other side, go round two sides of a playing field until you can take a rising path leading up to a main road. Cross the road, going left as far as a pathway, on the right, leading round the edge of a cemetery, which brings you out on another road. Turn right, go past the entrance to the cemetery, and a few strides later, turn left down a surfaced footpath between houses. Stay on this until, at the rear of a house it forks. Here branch right, and walk out to a road. Cross the road, going into another opposite to descend to Kingsland Bridge (27), where a toll of 1p is payable by pedestrians.

Over the bridge, at a junction (Town Walls), turn sharp right, doubling back down a walled alleyway to reach the River Severn. Turn left and follow the Severn beyond English Bridge (26), and finally, before reaching the railway bridge, turn left into St Mary's Water Lane. At the top of the lane bear right to reach the main street opposite Woolworths. Turn right and walk down towards the castle and the railway station. And the end of the walk.

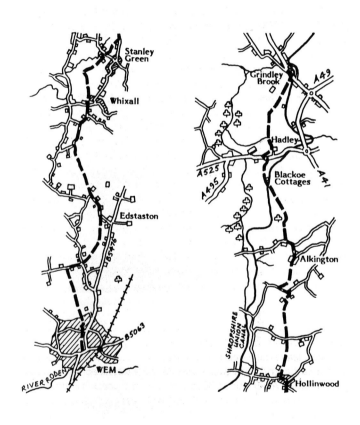

THE NORTHERN EXTENSION
NORTH – SOUTH

Grindley Brook to Wem
Distance: 16.5km (10¼ miles)

Grindley Brook is a canalside settlement on the Llangollen Canal, which started life in 1793 as the Ellesmere Canal, intended to link Shrewsbury with Liverpool via Ruabon, Chester and the Mersey. The planned route was much modified and it was finally operative from above Llangollen, through Ellesmere, along the north Shropshire border to Whitchurch and thence to join the Chester Canal near Nantwich. In 1811 it became the Ellesmere and Chester Canal and in 1846 became part of the Shropshire Union, or Shroppie, as it is affectionately known. After nationalisation in 1948 it gradually became known as the Llangollen Canal.

It was constructed by the Ellesmere Canal Company between 1793 and 1805, under the supervision of Thomas Telford, and the little Shropshire town of Ellesmere subsequently gave its name to the town which grew up around the Shroppie's Mersey terminus - Ellesmere Port. The Llangollen Canal was scheduled for closure in 1944, but somehow survived and is now one of our most popular waterways.

It enters the county at Grindley Brook via a flight of six locks, with the top three in a triple staircase. It has to be said that the canal is the only feature of interest at Grindley Brook, which straggles untidily alongside the A41. There are, however, facilities for refreshments and the surrounding pastoral countryside is green and pleasant.

The northern extension of the Shropshire Way begins from the Horse and Jockey pub at Grindley Brook, by setting off towards Whitchurch on the A41. Just after passing a small terrace of cottages, leave the A-road, on the right, at a signposted bridleway over a cattle grid, and then continue on a surfaced track across pastureland. After about 300m/yds, as the track swings right towards Bubney Farm, leave it and walk forward to the right of two oak trees, heading for a gate and stile ahead.

Cross the stile and go forward with a hedgerow on your left to another gate and stile, beyond which the Way continues along a field edge, with a hawthorn hedgerow on the left. This leads to another stile at a fence junction. Cross it and go forward with a fence then a hedgerow, on your left. When you reach the hedgerow, disregard the stile on the left, and keep forward to reach another gate/stile where you encounter a farm access.

Go left at the stile, descending slightly to a footbridge spanning a brook, Red Brook. Cross this and then bear half-left up the ensuing field towards the pole of an overhead power line. When you reach this, move slightly right to go up to Hadley Farm, and there keep forward through a gate/stile, with the buildings on your left. Just before reaching the farm access bear right to go past a slurry pit and then half-left across a field to reach Hadley Pool, and follow a fence around the pool to meet Wrexham Road (A525).

Cross the road with great care and join the track opposite, which takes you past Blackoe Cottages to a humpback bridge spanning the canal. Cross the bridge to enter a large arable field and walk diagonally to the top right corner, climbing slightly and enjoying good views of Ruabon Mountain and the border hills. A wobbly stile gives access to cattle pasture where you go forward beside the left-hand hedge to another stile at the far corner of the field. Turn right along the edge of the ensuing field but only for a short distance, until another stile enables you to enter the field on your right. The right of way goes diagonally across here, as indicated by the waymark, but you may find it blocked by impenetrable sweet corn. If so, follow the field boundary round to the left until you come to another stile.

Descend into a deep cutting, through which a railway once ran, cross the slippery footbridge at the bottom and climb out on the other side. Walk along the left-hand edge of the ensuing field then along the right-hand edge of the next. Join a lane opposite a farm (Fern Bank) and turn left, then first right on a narrow lane that is little more than a track.

This leads to the isolated hamlet of Alkington, where you turn right after Alkington House on a 'No through road' which takes you past Park Farm and straight through the yard to a gate into a cattle pasture. Continue forward, past a pond, then along the right-hand edge of two fields, passing a line of oak trees. A pair of stiles take you across an access track to join an enclosed track which leads into a meadow. Carry straight on along its right-hand edge to reach a lane where you turn left.

Take the first right, a 'No through road' which takes you to a farm. Keep straight on past it until a gate gives access to a meadow. Turn left, passing the farm, to find a gate into another meadow. Follow its right-hand edge to reach a large arable field. Keep straight on, now by the left-hand boundary, then along the edge of the next field to a lane.

Cross to an enclosed, and often overgrown, bridleway opposite that leads into a large cattle pasture. Head obliquely towards the far side, where you'll see a hunting gate midway along the hedge. Continue in much the same direction across another field, keeping to the left of Massey House Farm and joining its driveway close to a lane, where you turn left into Hollinwood.

Take the first right, by a village green, and keep straight on at a junction. Just after you pass a house named Rosannedd climb a stile on the right and go obliquely left past an oak tree to another stile. Go forward over another field, passing a pond, three oak trees and a timber-framed house, to reach a stile into the next field. Bear left to another stile and another field and keep on in much the same direction to a stile at the far side - if you can't immediately see it, just head towards a cluster of farm buildings which lie beyond it.

Cross a lane and walk down a 'No through road' opposite, passing Mill House Farm to enter a field. Follow the left-hand hedge for a short distance until it turns a corner. Don't go with it, but keep straight on across the field, passing to the right of a pond, to reach a stile at the far side. Go straight on along the left-hand edge of the ensuing arable field to the corner, where two stiles and a footbridge take you into a large pasture.

Go forward past a pond and straight on across this field and the next towards a farm. As you reach it, turn right to reach a stile between the farm buildings and a cream-painted house, Farthing Cottage.

Continue along a green lane to a road at Whixall and cross over to join a lane opposite. Fork right at the junction with Gilberts Lane, continue past Braynes Hall and fork left at the next junction. When the lane bends to the right, leave it to join a track on the left that leads into a meadow. Turn right along its edge and pass through a gap into the next field. Continue along its edge to a waymarked post by a pond and from this point go obliquely left to find a stile concealed in a hedge just to the left of another pond (on the other side of the hedge).

Climb over the stile and turn left on a path enclosed between a fence and a hedge. Ignore two branching paths and stay on the enclosed one, which eventually leads to a large arable field. Go forward by its left-hand hedge until the hedge turns a corner. Don't follow it, but maintain the same heading across the field, aiming for a stile near some hummocky earthworks. Go obliquely across an access track and then across a field to join the track. Follow it to a lane and turn left towards Edstaston.

Edstaston Bridge was designed by Thomas Telford and spans the course, long since filled in, of the Prees Branch of the Ellesmere Canal (part of the Shropshire Union system).

Join a footpath opposite the church of St Mary the Virgin, next to White Lodge.

Although it contains work from later periods, the Norman origins of this church are clearly displayed in the elaborate carvings around the three doors. Inside are some sensitively restored wall paintings and St Mary's is regarded as one of the county's finest churches. Edstaston itself is a scattered and unremarkable village, but it was a favourite of the playwright George Bernard Shaw, who was a frequent visitor.

Entering a field, go straight across to a stile at the far side. Continue across the next field, passing just to the left of a tree-fringed pond before going forward to a stile in the hedge ahead. Cross another field to a stile below an oak tree, and in the next field bear right to a stile beneath an ash tree.

Go obliquely right across the ensuing meadow, passing a pond and continuing to a stile next to a section of fence painted black and white. Climb over the stile and go forward along the right-hand edge of the next field.

A stile gives onto a lane, where you turn left, then immediately right. Just after passing a pond go over a stile on the left and follow a well-trodden path across fields, guided by a succession of stiles. Wem is now visible ahead and, beyond it, the tall spire of Clive Church pierces the sky from its commanding position on the western slopes of Grinshill Hill.

Eventually, a stile on your right gives access to a fenced and hedged path which leads to the edge of Wem and a surfaced path which turns right into an estate of bungalows. Turn left between numbers twenty-two and twenty-four and then keep straight on at a junction. Follow the street (Marlcroft) round to the right then go left at a T-junction onto Wemsbrook Road.

At the main road go straight across and join a narrow alleyway opposite (Drawwell Walk) which takes you into Wem, emerging on the main street by the Castle pub.

SOUTH – NORTH
Wem to Grindley Brook
Distance: 16.5km (10¼ miles)

At the top of Mill Street in Wem turn right on High Street and, immediately after passing the Castle pub, go left along a narrow alleyway, Drawwell Walk. This leads north, parallel with the main road (B5476) and brings you out on a residential street, which you cross to walk up Wemsbrook Road, almost opposite. Turn right into Marlcroft, at the end of which go left on a footpath which soon leaves the houses behind, continuing as a hedged and fenced path between fields grazed by cattle.

The path leads to a stile giving access to a field. Turn left along its edge then keep on in the same direction across a further six fields, guided by a fairly well-trodden path and a succession of waymarked stiles, to eventually reach a lane where you turn right.

Proceed to a T-junction and turn left, then cross the lane almost immediately to join a footpath. Follow the left-hand hedge the length of a field, over a stile at the far end and then diagonally left across another field towards a stile beneath a tall ash tree. Go left across the ensuing field, then right across the next one, guided by another waymarked stile.

Cross a large cornfield, passing just to the right of a tree-fringed pond, to reach a gate and stile at the far side, which give access to sheep pasture. Walk to the far right corner, passing close by a cottage to join a lane opposite the little church of St Mary the Virgin (168) at Edstaston.

Turn left along the lane, soon passing over Edstaston Bridge

(168). When the lane bends sharp left join the access track to The Park on the right. You very soon reach a gate, at which point you should look for a stile just to the right of it, concealed by tightly clipped conifers. Walk over a field then cross The Park's access track and go obliquely right to a stile into a large arable field.

Continue in the same direction to meet a hedge and follow it to the corner of the field where another stile gives access to a fenced and hedged footpath. When this eventually turns sharp left by a pond look for a stile hidden on the right. Go over here into a field and walk diagonally left to a waymarked post just to the right of a tree-fringed pond. Go forward to the field corner, through a gap into another field and on alongside the left-hand hedge to join a track leading to a lane.

Turn right, and, when you come to a junction, right again. Turn left at the next junction, just after Braynes Hall. At another junction, at Whixall, cross over to join a footpath. You may find it overgrown with nettles, as well as uneven underfoot, but persevere and you will find it soon improves. After passing Farthing Cottage climb a stile into a large field. Go forward past farm buildings, and turn left down-field to a gate and stile. Cross a further two fields to find a couple of stiles and a footbridge just beyond, and to the left of, a tree-fringed pond.

Cross into an arable field and turn right along its edge, into the corner, where an overgrown stile is concealed beneath a holly tree. Cross another field, keeping to the left of a pond, and at the far side join a track. Keep forward to pass Mill House Farm and reach a lane. Cross over and climb a stile into a field. Go straight ahead here, then bear very slightly left across another field to a concealed stile in the opposite hedge. Go forward across the next field and then diagonally right across one more, to reach a stile to the lane.

Turn left, and keep straight on at a junction to reach Hollinwood, where you turn left at a T-junction, signposted to Platt Lane and Whixall. At the entrance to Massey House Farm turn right, initially on the farm drive but almost immediately leaving it for a bridleway on the right. Follow it across a field, passing just to the right of the farm and through a hunting gate into a large pasture. Head for the far right corner, where a gate gives access to a fenced and hedged path, overgrown and uneven underfoot, which leads to a lane.

Cross over, entering a field opposite and following its right-hand edge, enjoying good views of the Welsh hills over to the west. At the top of the field go through a gate just to the left of a pond and carry on in the same direction. Pass through another gate at the top of the next field and bear left so that you pass just to the left of Fields Farm before turning right to join its access track. Follow this to a lane and turn left.

After about 300m/yds, as you approach a house with a roof of orange tiles, you'll see a pair of gates on the right. Concealed to the right of these is a stile – climb over to enter a meadow and follow the left-hand hedge to another stile beneath an oak tree. Continue along a green track, passing a plantation, then crossing a pair of stiles to enter another field. Follow its left-hand edge, and on along the edge of the next field, then through a gate to pass Park Farm.

Keep on along a lane for a short distance then take the first left, just after Alkington House. This quiet lane takes you to a junction where you turn left again. In a little under 200m/yds you will see two white gates on your right, opposite the barns at Fern Bank. Pass through the right-hand gate and follow the left-hand hedge to a stile, then along the edge of the next field until another stile allows you to cross to the other side of the hedge. Keep on in the same direction for a little way, then descend steps into a disused railway cutting, cross a slippery footbridge and climb out on the far side.

The route is now diagonally right across the next field, but you may find it obstructed by an impenetrable crop such as sweet corn. If this is the case, there is no option but to turn right and follow the field edge round until you come to a stile. Once over here turn left and you'll soon come to another stile on the left. Cross this into pasture and turn right along its edge.

Ignoring any branching paths, keep on in the same direction until you come to a stile that gives access to a sloping arable field. Go diagonally across here, passing just to the left of a solitary oak tree, and making for a canal bridge visible ahead.

A stile gives directly onto the bridge and, once across, turn right to join a track which passes Blackoe Cottages and leads to Wrexham Road.

Cross over and cross the roadside crash barrier beside Hadley Pool and the stile that immediately follows, and then go beside a fence around the pool towards the Hadley Farm buildings. As you reach the farm buildings, turn left and go through a gate and stile, continuing ahead to pass beneath power lines. From directly below the power lines branch half-left to a footbridge in the bottom corner of a field, spanning Red Brook.

Having crossed the footbridge go forward and climb easily into a shallow gully on a vehicle track at the top of which pass through a gate/stile and turn right to follow a hawthorn hedgerow on your right. When the hedgerow ends, at a stile, ignore the stile, and keep on in the same direction beside a fence and along field margins, always with either the fence or a hawthorn hedge on your right. This will guide you to an open pasture with Bubney Farm away to your left.

With hedgerows finally behind you go forward across a large pasture, aiming to the left of two oak trees, and soon reach a farm access which is followed forward and out to reach the A41. Turn left down the road and soon reach the end of the Shropshire Way at the Horse and Jockey pub.

WILD EDRIC'S WAY

It's a great name for a walk, but who exactly was Wild Edric? Well, we know he was a Saxon nobleman, probably an earl, who held a great deal of land, including the manors of Stoke (later Stokesay) and Clun, at the time of the Norman Conquest in 1066. Little more is known for certain about his background, although he seems to have been a member of an important family; one of his ancestors, Eadric, is thought to have been influential at the court of Ethelred the Unready, King of England from 978 until 1016.

After the Battle of Hastings, Edric declared allegiance to King William, but then thought better of it and was dispossessed as a consequence. As early as 1067 Richard le Scrob, of Richard's Castle (just to the south of Ludlow), was given the task of controlling Edric, who turned for assistance to the rulers of Powys and Gwynedd, Bleddyn and Rhiwallon, the half-brothers of Gruffudd ap Llywelyn, who had, from 1057 until 1063, been recognised as King of a briefly united Wales. Together Edric and the Welsh Princes took on and overcame the Norman garrison at Hereford. Encouraged by this victory, Edric then besieged Shrewsbury Castle in 1069, with a force of Welshmen and locals, augmented by a contingent from Cheshire. The castle held out, though much of the town was burnt before the rebels were repulsed.

Following Shrewsbury, it seems that Edric and William came to an agreement, but the details are unknown and, in any case, it didn't last long – some time between 1072 and 1085 Ralph de Mortimer was ordered to deal with Edric. What subsequently happened nobody knows.

There is no clear record of Edric's death, though Norman sources suggest he died in prison, while the Saxons claimed he died in action. Either claim might be true, or either might be nothing more than propaganda: for all we know, Edric might have become an outlaw and a bandit, or he might equally well have retreated to a quiet corner of Shropshire and made a living as a farmer.

It was probably inevitable that anybody who rebelled against Norman rule, however briefly, would become a folk hero to the downtrodden Saxons, and that is what happened to Edric, around whose memory successive generations wove increasingly unlikely stories. A complicated tangle of lore and legend developed, most of it based on Stiperstones (36-8), with the central story concerning the imprisonment of Edric and his followers in the lead mines beneath the ridge, and their emergence on horseback to tackle the enemy on those occasions when England is in danger. A Minsterley farmer reported seeing them just before the outbreak of the Crimean War and they had previously been seen before the Napoleonic Wars. Even in this century sightings were reported before both world wars.

The story has a very Arthurian twist to it (King Arthur and the Knights of the Round Table suffered the same fate), as does one of the more obscure legends about Edric, which tells how his sword lies in the reputedly bottomless Bomere Pool, guarded by a great fish. Bomere (which was the inspiration for Sarn Mere in Mary Webb's 'Precious Bane') lies between Shrewsbury and Condover, and it is said that the fish will not relinquish the sword until Condover Hall is inhabited by Edric's rightful descendants.

Whatever the facts of Edric's life and death, Wild Edric's Way is a terrific walk which takes in some of the finest Shropshire landscapes. But bear in mind that anyone witnessing Edric's spectral ride is said to be punished with either death or madness. So take care on crossing Stiperstones...

WILD EDRIC'S WAY

Wild Edric's Way is just under 79km (49 miles), across outstanding countryside, and can be comfortably completed in five days – Church Stretton – Bridges – Bishop's Castle – Clun – Craven Arms (Stokesay) – Ludlow.

CHURCH STRETTON TO BRIDGES
Distance: 9.5km (5.9 miles)

Church Stretton is a pleasant little town with a wonderful situation, a combination that has made it very popular with walkers. It became a minor spa in the nineteenth century when it was often enthusiastically referred to as 'Little Switzerland'. Naturally, it bears no more resemblance to Switzerland than any of the other British locations lumbered by the Victorians with this daft tag. It has no need of such comparisons anyway; Church Stretton and its hills have their own distinctive appeal. Immediately to the west of town rise the heathery slopes of the majestic Long Mynd (see page 34) while to the east are the shapely and seductive

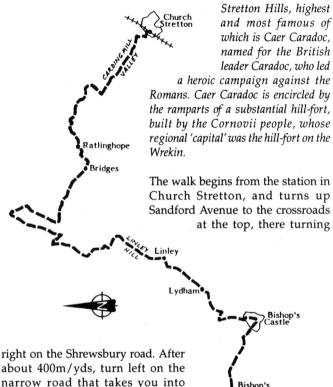

Stretton Hills, highest and most famous of which is Caer Caradoc, named for the British leader Caradoc, who led a heroic campaign against the Romans. Caer Caradoc is encircled by the ramparts of a substantial hill-fort, built by the Cornovii people, whose regional 'capital' was the hill-fort on the Wrekin.

The walk begins from the station in Church Stretton, and turns up Sandford Avenue to the crossroads at the top, there turning right on the Shrewsbury road. After about 400m/yds, turn left on the narrow road that takes you into Carding Mill Valley, an area now in the ownership of the National Trust.

There was a medieval corn mill in the valley, but in the nineteenth century a new 'carding' mill was constructed ('carding' is the process of combing wool fibres for spinning). Over the next fifty years, cottages and other buildings were erected in the valley for home spinners, dyers and weavers, but by the end of the century the mills had stopped working and been replaced by industries manufacturing ginger beer and soda water. A large 'tea room' was provided for visitors, and the National Trust still have a café here.

The way up the valley is never in doubt, and leads past a car park before starting to climb as a bridleway below Haddon Hill onto Motts Road, which was named after Charles Mott, a Church Stretton doctor who campaigned to get the bridlepath improved.

Gradually the path climbs onto the wide plateau of the Long Mynd where it meets a prominent track, the Portway.

The Portway was used as a drove road along which Welsh cattle were herded to English markets, but is almost certainly of Bronze Age origin, used by the early inhabitants of this region up to 4,000 years ago.

Turn right along the Portway until it forks. Branch left to reach a road. Follow this for about 700m/yds until, just after Wildmoor Pool, you can branch left on a descending path for Ratlinghope. The path brings you down to a fence that deflects you left to a stile. Cross this and go down the next field to a road. Turn left, following the road past Brow Farm at Ratlinghope (tea room (weekends only) and campsite), go past the road turning for Church Stretton, and finally turn right at a gate opposite Manor House. Further on you cross a bridge spanning a feeder of the River East Onny. Turn left after this and walk through woodland to meet a road once more, there turning right to walk down to Bridges.

BRIDGES TO BISHOP'S CASTLE
Distance: 19.7km (12¼ miles)

Go past the Bridges Youth Hostel and the Horseshoe Inn, and up to a road junction. Turn left and soon right onto an adjoining lane, and follow this up to Stedment. Here branch left for about 2km (1¼ miles) to go to the Stiperstones National Nature Reserve car park.

A little under 800m/yds then separates the car park and the next point at which Wild Edric's Way crosses this road. The route, however, prefers a 5km (3 miles) extension to include the main Stiperstones ridge, by going through a gate at the far end of the car park onto a track that sweeps across the hillside and through Gatten Plantation to the Hollies Farm, where it meets the Shropshire Way.

Between the Hollies Farm and Bishop's Castle, Wild Edric's Way exactly follows the Shropshire Way (as described on pages 36-44). There is, however, a minor variation which, when the route descends from Cranberry Rock to meet the road again, crosses the road and then immediately bears right, leaving the Shropshire Way, to head for a stile and an indistinct path descending parallel with overhead power lines to a fence corner and stile hidden in bracken and gorse. A continuing path leads down to The Bog Mines car park. This variant adds about 500m/yds to the distance.

Across the car park you emerge on a road again, and then reach The Bog, where there used to be up to twenty lead mines busily working away.

The Bog Mine was the focus of a community of some 200 people. It provided the main local employment for men and boys, while the women looked after the smallholdings around the cottages. The settlement developed steadily from the first major exploitation of the lead veins here in the 1740s. Lead mining ceased in the 1880s, but mining of barytes continued to the 1920s.

Despite the reputed richness of the lead vein at The Bog, mining here was not continuous. The lease for the mine changed hands frequently, and companies went bankrupt, leaving the workings to flood. When mining finally closed the mine had been sunk to a depth of 366m (1,200ft).

From The Bog, turn left up and along the road to Linley and More, only leaving it for a woodland track about 100m/yds after the turning for Brookshill Farm. This track brings you up to rejoin the Shropshire Way near Rock House.

BISHOP'S CASTLE TO CLUN
Distance: 17.5km (11 miles)

Walk down the main street in Bishop's Castle towards the church, and turn right at the Six Bells Inn onto Kerry Lane. Follow the lane (with care) for 2.8km (1¾ miles) to a road junction and there turn left to Bishop's Moat.

Keep straight on and, at the next junction, take the Pant Glas and Hopton road, which here follows the Kerry Ridgeway, until, after 3.4km (2 miles), you meet Offa's Dyke Path. Turn left over a stile and a few strides on another stile gives onto a path that bears left to run alongside the dyke. Eventually the route enters Nut

Wood and descends steeply to a farm track. Turn left along the track for about 100m/yds and then turn right over a footbridge, and go forward aiming for the obvious continuation of Offa's Dyke up the hillside ahead. Cross a fence corner by a stile, and climb beside

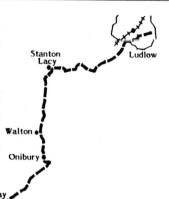

the on-going fence to go up and over Edenhope Hill before descending steeply to Churchtown. Cross the lane and climb a short distance on the other side to rejoin the Shropshire Way, as it emerges from Churchtown Wood, for the remaining stretch to Clun (as described on pages 49-51).

CLUN TO STOKESAY CASTLE (Craven Arms) Distance: 17.8km (11 miles)

Between Clun and Stokesay Castle, Wild Edric's Way faithfully follows the Shropshire Way (as described on pages 54-61), with just three minor deviations:

(1) Just after leaving Clun, having gone past the youth hostel and about 100m/yds further on, the Shropshire Way branches left beyond Lake Cottage to cut across a road bend: Wild Edric's Way stays on the road, and rejoins the Shropshire Way a few minutes later.

(2) Shortly after entering the plantation of Steppleknoll and Sunnyhill at a gate the Shropshire Way goes forward, climbing to meet a graded forestry track. Turn right along this and, when it forks, branch right (the Shropshire Way goes left). This variant simply takes you by an alternative forest trail onto the edge of Sunnyhill, emerging on the line of the Shropshire Way once more, just before it turns to go over Bury Ditches.

(3) Finally, having left Kempton on the rising track to Barlow House Farm, the Shropshire Way branches right to take a direct route to Hopesay. Wild Edric's Way stays on the farm access to pass the farm and continue to the Hopesay road about 500m/yds north of the turning (now left) onto Hopesay Hill.

STOKESAY CASTLE (Craven Arms) TO LUDLOW
Distance: 14.2km (9 miles)

Between Stokesay Castle and Ludlow, Wild Edric's Way exactly follows the Shropshire Way (as described on pages 62-68)

ESSENTIAL AND SUPPLEMENTARY READING

A Shropshire Gazetteer, Michael Raven (Michael Raven 1989)

Shropshire Countryside, Andrew Jenkinson (Minton & Minton 1990)

Shropshire's Wild Places: A Guide to the County's Protected Wildlife Sites, Andrew Jenkinson (Scenesetters 1992)

Shropshire (Shropshire County Council 1980)

An Illustrated Literary Guide to Shropshire, Gordon Dickins (Shropshire Libraries 1987)

Shropshire Hill Country, Vincent Waite (J M Dent & Son Ltd 1970)

Aspects of Shropshire, Shropshire County Council (Shropshire Books 1994)

Canals of Shropshire, Richard K Morriss (Shropshire Books 1991)

Borderlands, Julian Critchley and David Paterson (Peak Publishing Ltd)

The Buildings of England: Shropshire, Nikolaus Pevsner (Penguin Books 1958)

A Shropshire Lad, A E Housman (Palmers Press 1987)

Portrait of Shropshire, Brian J Bailey (Robert Hale Ltd 1981)

An Illustrated History of Shrewsbury, E J Priestley (Shrewsbury Borough Museums 1989)

The National Trust Countryside Handbook, Celia Spouncer (The National Trust 1993)

Exploring the West Midlands, Vivian Bird (Batsford 1977)

Walks around Telford, David Gregory (Shropshire Books 1995)

Ten Walks that Changed the World, Kate and Keith Pybus (Shropshire Books 1996)

Tea Shop Walks in Shropshire, Julie Meech (Sigma Leisure 1997)

The Shropshire Village Book, Shropshire Federation of Women's Institutes (Countryside Books/SFWI 1988)

The Trees of Shropshire, Andrew Morton (Airlife Publishing Ltd 1986)

The Old Parish Churches of Shropshire, Mike Salter (Folly Publications 1988)

The Castles and Moated Mansions of Shropshire, Mike Salter (Folly Publications 1988)

The Shropshire Hills, David Hunter (Cicerone Press 1991)

ACCOMMODATION GUIDE

This Accommodation Guide was compiled during 1998. It can only be updated further when the guide is reprinted. Meanwhile, walkers with information to add, or comments about any of the accommodation services mentioned, should contact the authors through the publisher. Such comments would be much appreciated.

The list of accommodation is not exhaustive, and is the product of a preliminary trawl of hotels, guesthouses, bed and breakfast establishments etc.. Not all of the entries provide all year opening, but welcome walkers, most provide evening meals and/or packed lunches, and where evening meals are not provided it is usually because there are excellent facilities in a nearby town or village. Most of the establishments that are more remote from the route of the Shropshire Way will provide a 'ferrying' and pick up service – do ask when making your arrangements.

CAMPSITES

There are few established campsites along the Shropshire Way, though many farmers will allow the odd tent or two for a night. To help preserve good relations with farmers, however, please make a point of obtaining permission before camping. In some cases, farmers actively encourage camping, though facilities are often basic.

Check the following list of B&B proprietors and youth hostels for (*), which indicates that the proprietor has some form of camping provision, but do make sure what facilities are on offer before committing yourself to staying there.

YOUTH HOSTELS

The following youth hostels are on or near the Shropshire Way. Full details of their opening times should be checked with the YHA Accommodation Guide.

Although you are able to book direct with any of the hostels, in Shropshire the YHA operates a Booking Bureau through which you can book all your accommodation (Shropshire Booking Bureau, Ironbridge Gorge YHA – see below).

(*) BRIDGES LONG MYND, Ratlinghope, Shrewsbury, Shropshire SY5 0SP (Tel/Fax: 01588 650656)

COALPORT, John Rose Building, High Street, Coalport, Shropshire TF8 7HT (Tel. 01952 588755 Fax: 01952 588722)

CLUN MILL, The Mill, Clun, near Craven Arms, Shropshire SY7 8NY (Tel/Fax: 01588 640582)

IRONBRIDGE GORGE, Paradise, Coalbrookdale, Telford, Shropshire TF8 7NR (Tel: 01952 433281 Fax: 01952 433166)

LUDLOW, Ludford Lodge, Ludford, Ludlow, Shropshire SY8 1PJ (Tel: 01584 872472 Fax: 01584 872095)

SHREWSBURY, The Woodlands, Abbey Foregate, Shrewsbury, Shropshire SY2 6LZ (Tel: 01743 360179 Fax: 01743 357423)

(*) WILDERHOPE MANOR, Longville in the Dale, Much Wenlock, Shropshire TF13 6EG (Tel: 01694 771363 Fax: 01694 771520)

BED AND BREAKFAST ACCOMMODATION

The following is a selection of accommodation available, based on information supplied by the proprietors. Ask if you are likely to want an evening meal, which in any case should always be booked in advance. Likewise, packed lunches.

Not all accommodation is directly on the Shropshire Way, so ask how far away the accommodation is first, and whether they offer a pick-up service.

To save space, the following entries are summarised. So, if you are writing to a proprietor then the full address is found by inserting the place heading (e.g. BISHOP'S CASTLE, Shropshire) immediately before the post code. The addresses are arranged to coincide with an anticlockwise circuit of the Way.

There are no entries for Shrewsbury; there are far too many establishments to list. Accommodation can be booked, however, by contacting the Tourist Information Centre at The Music Hall, The Square, Shrewsbury SY1 1LH (Tel. 01743 350761 Fax. 01743 355323)

RATLINGHOPE, Shrewsbury, Shropshire (Tel. Code 01588)
(*) Helen Sankey, Brow Farm, SY5 0SR (650641)

MINSTERLEY, Shrewsbury, Shropshire (Tel. Code 01743)
Paul Costello, Cricklewood Cottage, Plox Green, SY5 0HT (791229)

(*) Janet Higgins, Rowan House, Gravels Bank, SY5 0HG (891418)

(*) John Sproson, The Stiperstones Inn, Stiperstones, SY5 0LZ
(791327)

CHURCHSTOKE, Montgomery, Powys (Tel. Code 01588)
(*) Ceinwen Richards, The Drewin Farm, SY15 6TW (620325)

BISHOP'S CASTLE, Shropshire (Tel. Code 01588)
Ann Bennett, Bank House, High Street, SY9 5BQ (638146)
Jane Carroll, Old Time, 29 High Street, SY9 5BE (638467)
Geoff and Sue Grimes, The Poppy House, 20 Market Square,
SY9 5BN (638443)
(*) Rosita Hamar, Lagden Farm, Colebatch, SY9 5JY (638252)
Peter and Phyllis Hutton, The Old Brick Guesthouse,
7 Church Street, SY9 5AA (638471)
Grant Perry, The Boar's Head, Church Street, SY9 5AE (638521)
Ann Williams, Shuttocks Wood, Norbury, SY9 5EA (650433)
David Simpson, The Castle Hotel, The Square SY9 5BN (638403)

CLUN, Craven Arms, Shropshire (Tel. Code 01588)
Judy Bailey, Crown House, Church Street, SY7 8JW (640780)
Gill Della Casa, Birches Mill, SY7 8NL (640409)
(*) Miriam Ellison, New House Farm, SY7 8NJ (638314)
(*) Hurst Mill Farm (640224)
Mary Jones, Llanhedric, SY7 8NG (640203)
Mrs C Lewis, Clun Farm, SY7 8JB (640432)
The Sun Inn, 10 High Street, SY7 8JB (640559)
Bob and Margaret Wall, The Old Farmhouse, Woodside, SY7 0JB
(640695)
Sybil Waters, Hill House Farm, SY7 8LP (640325)
Roger Wren, Cockford Hall, SY7 8LR (640327)

KEMPTON, Lydbury North, Shropshire (Tel. Code 01588)
R Bright, Kempton Farm, SY7 0JG (660250)
Ann Evans, Brunslow Farm, SY7 8AD (680244)
(*) Hilary Evans, Walcot Farm, SY7 8AA (680243)
Mildred Goode, Lower Farmhouse, SY7 8AS (680230)

HOPESAY, Craven Arms, Shropshire (Tel. Code 01588)
Roger and Sheila Davies, Hesterworth, SY7 8EX (660487)

CRAVEN ARMS, Shropshire (Tel. Code 01588)
Jeff Aldridge, The Crown Inn, Newcastle, SY7 8OL (672304)

Janice Barrett, Pool House Farm, Clunbury, SY7 0HG (660414)
Mr D Parry, The Gables, Broome, SY7 0NX (660667)
Ray Rowley, Stokesay Castle Hotel, School Road, SY7 9PE (640271)
Janet Williams, The Firs, Norton SY7 9LS (672511)
Brian and Lynn Willis, Hill View, Clun Road, SY7 9QW (672619)

ONIBURY, Nr Craven Arms, Shropshire (Tel. Code 01584)
(*) Vivienne Parry, Onibury Station House, SY7 9AZ (856336)

LUDLOW, Shropshire (Tel. Code 01584)
Tony Banks, Blue Boar, Mill Street (872630)
Greg Biggerton, Dinham Hall, SY8 1EJ (876464)
Mrs J S Bowen, Arran House, 42 Gravel Hill, SY8 1QR (873764)
The Charlton Arms, Ludford Bridge (872813)
Stuart Copland, The Church Inn, Butter Cross, SY8 1AW (872174)
Clare and David Currant, Corndene, Coreley, SY8 3AW (890324)
(*) Nigel and Ailish Halford, The Hen and Chickens, 103 Old
    Street, SY8 1NU (874318)
Hucks Barn Farm, Overton Road, SY8 4AA (873950)
Maggie Hughes, The Compasses Kitchen, The Compasses,
    1 Corve Street, SY8 1DA (872967)
Mrs Valerie Humphreys, Seifton Court, Culmington, SY8 2DG
    (861214)
Roger and Helen Jones, The Cliffe Hotel, Dinham, SY8 2JE (872063)
Philip Maile, Bull Hotel, 14 Bull Ring, SY8 1AD (873611)
John and Sybil McColgan, Emerald Guest House, 111 Old Street,
    SY8 1NU (872496)
Patricia Ross, Number Twenty Eight, 28 Lower Broad Street,
    SY8 1PQ (876996)

KNOWBURY, Ludlow, Shropshire (Tel. Code 01584)
Annie Felix, Redthorpe Villa, SY8 3JL (890638)

CLEEDOWNTON, Ludlow, Shropshire (Tel. Code 01584)
Bernadette Chivers, The Moor Hall, SY8 3EG (823209)

ABDON, Shropshire (Tel. Code 01746)
Rex and Jutta Langham, Spring Cottage, SY7 9HU (712551)

HUGHLEY, Nr Shrewsbury, Shropshire (Tel. Code 01746)
(*) Mill Farm Holiday Park, SY5 6NT (785208)

[WILDERHOPE]
LONGVILLE IN THE DALE, Much Wenlock, Shropshire
(Tel. Code 01694)
Mrs Dixon, Wilderhope Farm, TF13 6EG (771285)

MUCH WENLOCK, Shropshire (Tel. Code 01952)
Susan Green, The Old Police Station, Sheinton Street, TF13 6HU
    (727056)
The Plume of Feathers, Harley, SY5 6LP (727360)
Maxine Sheldon, Gaskell Arms Hotel, TF13 6AQ (727212)
Nan Thorpe, Old Quarry Cottage, Brockton, TF13 6JR (785596)

BROSELEY, Shropshire (Tel. Code 01952)
Diane Kaiser, Orchard House, 40 King Street, TF12 5NA (882684)
Stephen McNally, Lord Hill Guest House, Duke Street,
    TF12 5LU (884270/580792)
Laurie Nixey, Broseley Guest House, The Square, TF12 5EW
    (882043)
Gordon and Marilyn Selway, Rock Dell, 30 Ironbridge Road,
    TF12 5AJ (883054)

IRONBRIDGE, Telford, Shropshire (Tel. Code 01952)
Calcutts House, Calcutts Road, Jackfield, TF8 7LH (882631)
(*) The Firs Guest House, 32 Buildwas Road, TF8 7BJ (432121)
George Maddocks, The Library House, Severn Bank, TF8 7AN
    (432299)
Bill and Ev Morgan, Ye Olde Robin Hood Inn,
    33 Waterloo Street, TF8 7HQ (433100)
Post Office House, 6 The Square, TF8 7AQ (433201)
Nita Reed, Severn Lodge, New Road, TF8 7AS (432148)
Mrs M Richards, Woodlands Farm, Beech Road, TF8 7PA (432741)
Maxine Roberts, Wharfage Cottage, 17 The Wharfage, TF8 7AW
    (432721)
Tontine Hotel, The Square, TF8 7AL (432127)

COALBROOKDALE, Telford, Shropshire (Tel. Code 01952)
June Ashdown, Coalbrookdale Villa, 17 Paradise, TF8 7NR (433450)

LITTLE WENLOCK, Telford, Shropshire (Tel. Code 01952)
Mrs L M Lee, Coppice Heights, Spout Lane, TF6 5BL (505655)

HIGH ERCALL, Telford, Shropshire (Tel. Code 01952)
Maryke Stansfield, The Old Vicarage, Shop Lane, TF6 6AG (770616)

ASTLEY, Shrewsbury, Shropshire (Tel. Code 01939)
W and A R Tudor, Holly Farm, SY4 4BP (210446)

SHAWBURY, Shropshire (Tel. Code 01939)
Mrs M L Woodcock, Unity Lodge, Moreton Mill, SY4 4ES (250831)

PRESTON BROCKHURST, Shrewsbury, Shropshire (Tel. Code 01939)
(*) Janet Jones, Grove Farm, SY4 5QA (220223)

WEM, Shropshire (Tel. Code 01939)
Barbara Barnes, Foxleigh House, Foxleigh Drive, SY4 5BP (233528)
Mr and Mrs C Brown, Polstead House, Shawbury Road,
    SY4 5PF (233530)
Anne James, Forncet, Soulton Road, SY4 5HR (232996)
Ann Jones, Lowe Hall Farm, SY4 5UE (232236)
Anne Peel, Chez Michael, 23 Roden Grove, SY4 5HJ (232947)
Clive Shingler, Lower Lacon Caravan Park (232376)

GRINSHILL, Shrewsbury, Shropshire (Tel. Code 01939)
Barrie Jones, Elephant and Castle Inn, SY4 3BL (220410)

(*) Signifies that the proprietor makes some provision for camping, but
check exactly what, first.

INDEX

IF YOU LIKE ADVENTUROUS ACTIVITIES ON
MOUNTAINS OR HILLS
YOU WILL ENJOY

Climber

MOUNTAINEERING / HILLWALKING /
TREKKING / ROCK CLIMBING /
SCRAMBLING IN BRITAIN AND ABROAD

*AVAILABLE FROM NEWSAGENTS,
OUTDOOR EQUIPMENT SHOPS,
OR BY SUBSCRIPTION
(6-12 MONTHS) from*

**MYATT McFARLANE PLC
PO BOX 28, ALTRINCHAM, CHESHIRE WA14 2FG
Tel: 0161 928 3480   Fax: 0161 941 6897
ISDN No: 0161 926 8937   e-mail: mmpe-mail@aol.com**

THE WALKERS' MAGAZINE

COMPULSIVE MONTHLY READING FOR
ANYONE INTERESTED IN WALKING

*AVAILABLE FROM NEWSAGENTS,
OUTDOOR EQUIPMENT SHOPS, OR BY SUBSCRIPTION
(6-12 MONTHS) from*

**CALEDONIAN MAGAZINES LTD,
6th FLOOR, 195 ALBION STREET, GLASGOW G1 1QQ
Tel: 0141 302 7700 Fax: 0141 302 7799
ISDN No: 0141 302 7792   e-mail: info@calmags.co.uk**

mountain / sports incorporating 'Mountain INFO'

Britain's liveliest and most authorative magazine for mountaineers, climbers and ambitious hillwalkers. Gives news and commentary from the UK and worldwide, backed up by exciting features and superb colour photography. *OFFICIAL MAGAZINE*

Have you read it yet?

Available monthly from your newsagent or specialist gear shop.

Call 01533 460722 for details

BRITISH MOUNTAINEERING COUNCIL